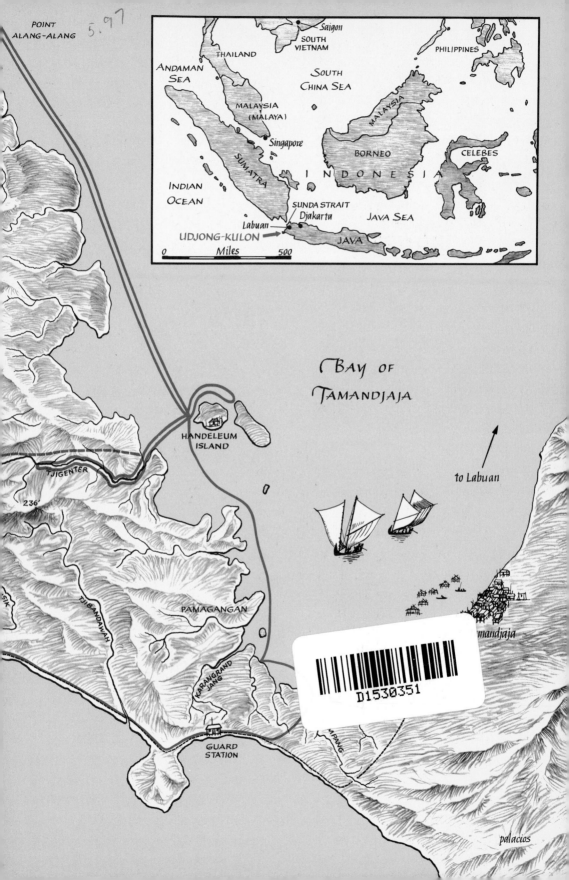

POINT
ALANG-ALANG

5.97

Saigon
SOUTH
VIETNAM
THAILAND
PHILIPPINES
ANDAMAN
SEA
SOUTH
CHINA SEA
MALAYSIA
(MALAYA)
MALAYSIA
Singapore
BORNEO
CELEBES
SUMATRA
I N D O N E S I A
INDIAN
OCEAN
SUNDA STRAIT
Djakarta
Java Sea
Labuan
UDJONG-KULON
JAVA
0   Miles   500

BAY of
TAMANDJAJA

to Labuan

HANDELEUM
ISLAND

TJIGENTER

236'

Tamandjaja

PAMAGANGAN

TJIBANDAWAH

SIK

KARANGRAND
JANG

MPANG

GUARD
STATION

palacios

JAVA DIARY

JAVA DIARY

by ELIOT ELISOFON

THE MACMILLAN COMPANY
COLLIER-MACMILLAN LTD., LONDON

FIRST PRINTING

The Macmillan Company
Collier-Macmillan Canada Ltd., Toronto, Ontario
Printed in the United States of America

To my brother Edward

Acknowledgments

JAVA DIARY is the story of my search for a rare animal, the *Rhinoceros sondaicus,* a one-horned rhinoceros that is almost extinct. The estimated twenty or so that survive are all on the western tip of Java, in a nature reserve called Udjong Kulon where I spent about three months in 1967.

I went there to do a photo-essay for *Life* magazine, and I wish to thank Patricia Hunt, Richard Pollard, and Ralph Graves, the nature, picture, and edition editors respectively of that magazine, for selecting me for the assignment.

A photographer on assignment for *Life* magazine is supported by many of its staff. Those in the photographic laboratory are most important, and among them George Karas, Herbert Orth, Hank Ehlbeck, Al Schneider, and John Francis should be specially noted. Also due thanks is Jeanne Warne of the Time Inc. travel department.

Special thanks are due to Charles A. Lindbergh, who urged *Life* to do this story after his visit to Udjong Kulon earlier that year, and for allowing me to publish his letter to *Life.*

My debt to the Smithsonian Institution of Washington, D.C., is great. Dr. S. Dillon Ripley, the Secretary of the Smithsonian, was kind enough to allow Dr. Lee M. Talbot, Field Representative for International Affairs in Ecology and Conservation, to accompany me to Udjong Kulon, a sanctuary he had visited four times before, to acquaint me with the terrain and its animals. I have written so much about Dr. Talbot in the text that it is sufficient to say here that this book would never have been accomplished without his guidance. In addition, his wife, Marty, a Research Associate at the Smithsonian, has helped coordinate the assistance of the botanists and zoologists of the Smithsonian's Museum of Natural History in identifying some of the flora and fauna of the sanctuary. Dr. George Watson, chairman of the Smithsonian's Department of Vertebrate Zoology, and his staff were kind enough to identify some of the birds of Udjong Kulon from the photographs I made.

Many people in Indonesia were helpful and I thank them all. In particular, U.S. Ambassador Marshall Green and Mr. Robert Keith, Mr. Edward Barber, and Miss Deirdre Ryan of his staff. Mr. Amir Daud, the *Time-Life* stringer in Djakarta, and his assistant, Tommy Graciosa, were helpful on a very professional level, as well as Kumar, their driver. Mr. Werner Milfeld, the assistant manager of the Hotel Indonesia, managed to accommodate me at any time I came through.

Udjong Kulon is administered through a complex government structure of science, forests, and game conservation involving many distinguished scientists, all of whom were helpful. I wish to mention Professor Sarwono, Doctor Soemarwoto, Doctor Sudjarwo, Doctor Basjarudin, Doctor Suhadi, and Mr. Made Taman.

Several members of the game conservation department were active participants in our project: game warden Djuhari in charge of Udjong Kulon, and game warden Sinaga, who worked closely with me, as well as Effendy Abdoessoeki, who took leave from his post at Bandung University to accompany me when Sinaga left. My warmest thanks are extended to the various farmers, fishermen, and sailors who were my crew in the sanctuary, chopping open trails, tracking animals, building shelters, carrying gear, and all the other tasks necessary to an operation of this type.

Mr. Benjamin Galstaun, the director of the Djakarta Zoo, and his charming wife, Henriette, were not only very helpful professionally, but were the most hospitable people I encountered in Indonesia.

My task was made considerably easier and certainly more pleasant by the assistance, advice, and company of Professor Doctor Rudolf Schenkel, a Swiss animal behavior scientist from Basle University, and his wife, Lotte, who were in Udjong Kulon studying the rhinoceros through a grant from the World Wildlife Fund.

The cooperation of the Indonesian government was essential and His Excellency Sultan Buwono personally participated in this, as well as his assistant, Sri Budojo. Nitour, the government tourist agency, was also helpful.

Finally I wish to thank Dorothea Scher, my secretary and assistant in New York, who patiently struggled with various pieces of handwritten manuscript which came out of the sanctuary and who tolerated my periods of bad temper when the strain became too much for me. Ralph Graves, Arthur A. Cohen, and Maitland Edey were kind enough to read the manuscript and offer advice. I wish to thank Mr. Ulrich Ruchti of Chanticleer Press for designing this book, and Mrs. Ellen Hsiao, who assisted him. I also thank my two teen-age daughters, Elin and Jill, who inspired the writing of this diary as letters to them that grew into a book.

ELIOT ELISOFON

Introductory Letter

Scotts Cove
Darien, Connecticut
June 11, 1967

Mr. Ralph Graves
Miss Patricia Hunt
Editorial Department
Life
Time & Life Building
New York, New York

Referring to my letter to Sri Budojo, a copy of which I mailed to you yesterday, it would of course be possible for your photographic expedition to get along without a full-time boat. But I think this would be of doubtful wisdom. There is at present not even radio communication with the Udjong Kulon bases and guard stations, and without a boat available neither medical assistance nor any supplies required could be obtained (at least under normal circumstances) in less than several days. As I recall, it is about a three-day paddle and walk from the base at Peutjang island to phone communication with Djakarta. Also, I would be hesitant to rely too much on the return schedule arranged with any boat engaged on a temporary basis.

As I said during our lunch meeting Thursday, if better arrangements cannot be made, I think a fishing boat, with engine, might be adequate, although slow. Starting from the harbor at Labuan (a four-hour car trip from Djakarta), a fishing boat should be able to make the voyage to Peutjang island in ten or twelve hours. (It should be borne in mind that the harbor at Labuan has deteriorated to a point where a boat can get in or out only at high tide, and not always then.) A fishing boat could be rented, I was told, for about $20 U.S. per day plus fuel. Part of the deck is usually roofed; but photographic equipment should be well protected against storm and spray. (The record of damage to photographic equipment in the Udjong Kulon area from salt water and from humidity is bad.)

Aside from catching fish, which cannot always be relied upon, no food supplies are available in the Udjong Kulon area. An expedition should be completely self-sustaining in this respect. Water is available from wells and streams, but should be boiled wherever human habitation is in the vicinity. (I drank water freely from the jungle streams.) There is some malaria in Labuan, but little if any in Udjong Kulon at present, I was told. Regular antimalaria dosages are advisable.

Weather was hot by day, but I found it not oppressively so (month of May). I always used a blanket before the night was over. There are two buildings at the Peutjang island base, but they were overcrowded at the time I was there. I slept on a split-bamboo floor of the building used by the guards. On the mainland opposite the island is a watchtower, well ventilated and plenty large enough for your photographic expedition. It was unused during my visit; but the area surrounding it is to be cleared of brush about this time, and plans call for the workmen (about ten) to live in the watchtower while the clearing is under way. I suggest that your expedition consider using this tower as headquarters, and that inquiry be made as to its availability.

It would be possible, although probably pretty crowded, to base on the boat you use. (Incidentally, the expedition will need a small boat to get back and forth from shore.) But I think it would be advisable to take bugproof tents as a back-up. (Bugs weren't bad when I was there, but Dr. Talbot says they are at times.) The tents should have plenty of ventilation openings, and I suggest a double roof. Of course, knives are necessary for cutting through jungle. The usual medicines and first-aid supplies should be carried. I prefer desert boots for walking. Some like canvas shoes.

Much personal equipment is not essential. I had not planned on a jungle expedition, and in addition to regular business clothing, had only a pair of khaki slacks. It was enough for the two weeks I spent there; but the jungle is thorny, and clothing is torn quickly. Extra clothing would simplify washing and drying in wet weather. For observing animals, I suggest a camouflage uniform similar to that used by jungle troops— advantageous but not essential.

I advise strongly that anyone going on this expedition have initiative, tact, patience, and flexibility. As far as scientific and detailed information is concerned, you could not find a better man than Lee Talbot to advise you. He is one of the best in the business, and he knows Udjong Kulon much better than I do.

I would think that the blind for photographing rhino should be priority one on its list after the expedition arrives in Udjong Kulon. (This raises a problem of material and labor that should be considered in advance.) It may take the animals a little time to get accustomed to the blind after its erection. Possibly more than one blind should be set up. I think of rhino wallows for a location, and a wide grass strip running from a landing to the Udjong Kulon lighthouse as another location. (This strip contained numerous rhino tracks last month.) But Dr. Talbot can give you still better advice here. And in Indonesia you can get excellent advice from Professor and Mrs. (Dr.) Schenkel of the World Wildlife Fund expedition—I think the best advice available there in regard to the rhinoceros and their current location. Chief Game Warden Djuhari, of the Udjong Kulon area, is a highly capable man. He works closely with the Schenkels, speaks a little English, Dutch somewhat better.

Professor and Mrs. Schenkel can be reached by mail through the Swiss Embassy in Djakarta, but they are sometimes out of contact for weeks at a time. They can probably always be located either through the Swiss Embassy or by sailing along the coasts of the Udjong Kulon and watching for their boat and base.

I suggest that you consider Peutjang island for your photographic and descriptive base. (Living in the watchtower on the mainland opposite would not preclude this.) It is a roundish, jungle-covered island lying a few hundred yards off the northwest coast of the Udjong Kulon's bulbous peninsula. I have never before seen such juxtaposition of growths of land and sea. Stepping out of a mat-walled dwelling in the base-camp clearing, you are within one minute's walk of a white-sand beach which slopes into crystal water. Across the beach and a neck of ocean are the spongy-green hills, hidden streams, and mud wallows of the few remaining Javanese rhinoceros— called "badak" by Indonesians.

Once in the water, with its sense of coolness stirred by beating sun, it takes less than five minutes' swimming to reach some of the most spectacular fish and coral formations of the South Pacific—thousands of tropical fish, a seemingly infinite variety of sea plants and corals—combinations of previously unimaginable shapes, colors, and shadings. You see great gaping jaws of shells; starfish, blue and red; darting movements and flashing scales; the placid immobility of sea cucumbers. Every stroke of your arms brings a scene change; every glance something new, like the twist of a kaleidoscope. You feel that on no galaxy could be concocted more fantastic life; yet you yourself are a part of it.

Turning inland instead of seaward from your dwelling, you are almost immediately in the daylong twilight of high-branched jungle. Grotesquely twisting vines, of python width, tangle through multitrunked trees that have diameters often exceeding our largest redwoods. Small birds call constantly. Peacocks screech, and the heavy swish of hornbill wings overhead marks life in an unseen sky. Frequent areas of jungle floor, in their leaf shade, are clear of brush and plants. Walking quietly over the soft loam you see families of wild pigs running, rooting about, and squealing in their quarrels. Monkeys swing overhead. A giant lizard staggers onto a log and gawks. Deer bark and look at you curiously before retreating into brush. You can probably find a real python if you press the hunt.

Lying on a sea edge in evenings, you watch flying foxes ply back and forth between island and mainland—giant bats with wingspreads of a yard or more, dozens, sometimes hundreds at a time, flapping slowly against the wind, flexing and bobbing in its gusts, sometimes dropping low enough to touch the water. You feel inverted from the modern to a Mesozoic age. Night falls quickly seven degrees south of the equator. Bird calls stop. The flying foxes diminish in number. The island's wildlife appears to be settling down for night. A chanting by the Indonesian guards begins. But as hours pass, and lanterns go out, and the chanting ends, shadows move from jungle into the base's clearing—deer, young pigs, an occasional snake. Their eyes glow and they vanish quickly if you throw a torch beam on them. You then realize that the neatness of the green and well-mowed lawn is kept by wild animals, not men.

The next day, an hour's voyage in a dugout canoe (purchased for the equivalent of $40 U.S., complete with paddles, mast, and sail) will bring you and seven others to a mainland landing which serves the Udjong Kulon lighthouse—the only permanent human habitation in the reserve, aside from guard posts. From this landing, a cleared grass-covered strip through jungle extends roughly a mile to the lighthouse promontory. It is covered by the tracks of wild cattle, deer, and rhinoceros. The coconut-lined path in the center of this strip ends at the canting steps, tumbling brick walls, and rusting iron of an old Dutch lighthouse.

You climb a long flight of steps to the top of the promontory and somewhat better surviving buildings of the ancient lighthouse. Here, isolated for weeks on end, the keeper and his family maintain their routine ways and tend a modern flashing beacon for night-passing ships. About fifty miles northeastward is the glowing volcano Anak Krakatau, island memorial of one of man's greatest nature-caused disasters. Southward, edging out from the Indian Ocean's foamy high-rock coast, waters extend nearly islandless for some four thousand miles to the Antarctic continent.

Turning southeastward, and looking over lighthouse ruins, you know that less than a mile away (but maybe requiring days of thorn-impeded tracking time to find them) are rhinoceros, huge creatures whose terrifying snorts and jungle crashings screen their shyness. They are near extermination by the hand of man. A few years ago, Javanese tigers roamed the same jungles. Now they have been reduced to doubtful rumors surrounding interior and seldom-penetrated mountains—to the unconfirmed report of a dung pile, or of a pad print over leopard size.

The Udjong Kulon, hanging geographically by a thread to the western tip of Java, symbolizes the desperation of many of our planet's animals. In it the life-or-death battle for survival of a distinct species of rhinoceros is being fought. It preserves a variety of Indonesian fauna and flora in a remnant of primary forest that once covered most of Java. Here, as in other critical areas of wilderness on every continent, modern man is confronted by the startling values of nature his civilization so facilely destroys. And here will be decided to a large degree whether man continues to exterminate his planet's wildlife or preserves at least the seeds for future use. The field base and scientific research station on Peutjang island, where representatives of all countries can meet in the interest of nature conservation, should play a major role in the answer. This is among my reasons for suggesting that you consider the island for your expedition's base.

Sincerely,

CHARLES A. LINDBERGH

JAVA DIARY

It was a hot June night and I was asleep in a fifth-floor apartment of the Château Marmont, an old Hollywood hotel that's become an institution for Broadway people coming to California to work in films. At 7 A.M. the telephone woke me.

It was Richard Pollard, the picture editor of *Life,* offering me first refusal on an assignment he felt I'd want to do. Senior men, even those on full staff (I have been on contract for the last three years, after twenty years on staff), are never ordered to do a particular assignment; they're invited to, and sometimes, for one reason or another, refuse. But not very often.

This assignment was an essay for the 1967 year-end double issue, *The Wild World.* Other photographers were already at work in Africa, Australia, the Arctic, and elsewhere. I could have the wildlife of Indonesia—in a Javanese nature reserve called Udjong Kulon.

Pollard knew I was hard at work on a picture book, *The Hollywood Style*—movie critic and historian Arthur Knight was writing the text—for publication by Macmillan in 1969. But he also knew me, and my love for this kind of story. At stake was the almost immediate stopping of work in Hollywood homes, and also giving up my forthcoming vacation, which was to include a month with my daughters, Elin and Jill, at my country home on Vinalhaven, an island in Maine's Penobscot Bay. This was asking a lot, and I couldn't answer at 7 A.M. I'd think it over, I told Pollard, and call him back. First, I had to square this with my daughters. I shouldn't have worried. Elin, then fifteen, said that I'd never be happy in Maine that summer knowing someone else was doing the Java story. Jill agreed, and so did my former wife, and still best friend, Joan. Then I had to explain to Arthur Knight and to Peter Ritner, Macmillan's editor-in-chief. I promised to come back from Java in time to complete the Hollywood book before January 1, when it had to go to press. All this took a few hours, and I was on.

I didn't pack my bags that day. In spite of my enthusiasm, I finished that week's appointments, some with people who wouldn't have extended another invitation, and then I flew to New York. Patricia Hunt, *Life's* able and very dedicated nature editor, wanted me to leave for Java immediately because color pages for the year-end issue had to be closed by November 1 at the latest. *Life* can engrave and print color in a few days, and does so at great expense on fast-breaking news—but not for an issue on the wilderness.

There were still July, August, September, and October, I argued, four months to go to Java and do the story; and I wanted the first two weeks of July in Maine with my girls. At first it didn't seem as if I'd get the time. Then, finally, it was made possible, for the editors decided that Dr. Lee M. Talbot, a leading wildlife ecologist from the Smithsonian, should accompany me to Java, at least for the first two or three weeks—and Dr. Talbot was then in South America and couldn't leave before the end of July, which was perfect for me.

Lee Talbot had already made two visits to Udjong Kulon, the last one in 1964, and most important, he knew all the Indonesian government officials involved in game conservation and would help arrange all my permissions, which could be very difficult. Larry Burrows, one of *Life's* best staff photographers, who works out of the Orient, had gone there alone earlier in the year, and run into a lot of bureaucratic flak. He was back in New York for consultation on his assignment—wildlife in Indonesia—and just then was named the News Photographer of the Year by the University of Missouri School of Journalism annual contest. Now *Life* needed him for a month-long national drum-beating tour for the magazine.

Burrows was not too unhappy to give up the Indonesia assignment. He explained the impossible logistics of a nation scattered over so many islands, and the editors, having the enthusiastic letter of Charles Lindbergh, who had visited Udjong Kulon in

May, decided with me to limit the story to just that one sanctuary. The fact that I was second choice for the story didn't bother me one bit. I was thrilled to go.

The preparations for the trip were not very different from preparations for the odd dozen previous trips I'd made to Africa and New Guinea, and I had lots of gear. I still had to refurbish personal and camping equipment, and most important, choose the color films and cameras I'd take with me. I decided on Kodachrome II for well-lit scenes in which strong color was needed, and high-speed Ektachrome for dark under-the-trees photography with softer contrast. There was no choice on cameras. I would take four Nikon F's, the best single-lens reflex 35mm camera made, and with these a whole battery of lenses. A particular problem was which extreme telephotos to take. All magazine photographers own most of their own equipment, and I had a 300mm and 500mm of my own. These provided six- and ten-times magnification. I borrowed a 1000mm mirror lens (20X magnification) from the *Life* stockroom and took the long lenses with me to Maine to practice.

Using equipment as specialized as this needs not only aptitude but familiarity, and I spent an hour or more every day trying to keep sea gulls in focus. I also worked on sailboats, somewhat easier. I tried both hand-held and tripod setups to learn what I could hold steady at which shutter speeds. I also was testing the color quality of both films, since they vary constantly. I was glad I did because I discovered that this Kodachrome had a greenish cast. *Life's* John Francis, who runs the stockroom, searched all over New York for an older emulsion, which had tested out okay. *Life* keeps a color chart on each emulsion it stocks, so photographers can see its characteristics —but I also make my own tests before a major assignment.

I left New York at the end of July and met Talbot for the first time face to face at the Paris airport. I had gone to Scotland for a few days en route, and he had stopped briefly in Washington on his way to Djakarta. I picked him out in the waiting room immediately, although no one had described him to me. Conservatively dressed in a Washington seersucker uniform, he had the look of a man who knew where he was going —quiet and confident, with a brush haircut, a slightly upturned nose, ears that did not lie flat against his skull, and the quickest, sharpest blue eyes I've ever seen; his complexion showed that it had felt lots of wind and sun.

We discovered that we had not only a host of mutual friends, but mutual likes and dislikes of almost everything. Both of us are ardent conservationists. I knew we were going to get along. We had to, if my assignment in Java was ever to succeed.

Talbot and I had plently of time, once we boarded the plane, to talk about Udjong Kulon, the largest animal preserve and also the rarest. I learned some more about my principal target there, the Javan rhinoceros, also called the lesser one-horned rhinoceros. Talbot believed that two dozen is a conservative estimate of the number left of this species, and all of them are in Udjong Kulon. There are no elephants, once common throughout Southeast Asia, and although there are leopards, no one has seen any tigers in the reserve during the last decade. There are many other species of flora and fauna that Talbot believed would make ample subjects for my camera.

I mentioned to him my interest in animal illustrations and that the earliest picture of a rhinoceros that I knew of was the animal engraved on a seal found in Mohenjo Daro, a civilization of three millennia B.C. on the Indus River. Another early illustration was Albrecht Dürer's wood engraving of the rhinoceros which reached Lisbon in 1513, having been sent there to King Manoel of Portugal by an Indian ruler.

Talbot was pleased that I had considerable experience with the African black rhinoceros, once described by Hemingway as antediluvian. The open grasslands of East Africa where this animal lives are very suitable for photography from four-wheel-drive vehicles. The photograph of one of these animals [which I reproduce here] was taken near Mt. Kilimanjaro in 1947 with

This African black rhinoceros charging at Amboseli, Kenya, was photographed in 1947.

a famous white hunter, Donald Ker, at the wheel of a truck. We allowed the rhino to charge us and then Ker made an almost ninety-degree right turn to allow me to catch the animal in full profile. There are no open grasslands in Udjong Kulon and no vehicles.

There are actually five different species of rhinoceros existing today, three in Asia and two in Africa. Besides the black one, the white rhinoceros lives in the White Nile area of the Southern Sudan. I once visited a town there called Rhino Camp, so named because Teddy Roosevelt shot specimens of this animal in that region for the American Museum of Natural History.

Of the three Asiatic species, only one has two horns like those of both the African species. This is the Sumatra rhinoceros. The other two have single small horns usually less than three quarters of a foot long. The Indian greater one-horned rhinoceros and the Javan lesser one-horned rhinoceros look very much alike. The slightly smaller one has a continuous fold of hide across the body in front of the shoulders while the Indian one has an interrupted fold. All three Asiatic species have their smooth, almost hairless hides divided by these deep folds at several points of the body and the tops of the legs giving the appearance of a heavy jacket of armor. Only the Asiatic species have very powerful sharp-edged incisor and canine teeth which they use as weapons.

The five species have one important element in common— they are in danger of extermination. Some men hunt them for the foolish and vain glory of having killed the animals with high-powered rifles, and others for the money obtained for the horns. These horns are not bone or part of the skull structure, but are agglutinated stiff hairs hardened like a horn. Used as a poison-detector cup in ancient times, powdered rhino horn is now considered by the Chinese the most potent male aphrodisiac, and a large horn will bring several thousand dollars in the market.

We flew directly to Djakarta. The only event was at Singapore, when we picked up a beautiful Swedish kerosene refrigerator, which was waiting on the field as luggage, courtesy of Peter Simms, the *Time-Life* correspondent there, who had answered my cabled query about these machines. To say that I surprised the customs men in Djakarta with a crated 4½-cubic-foot refrigerator in my luggage is to put it mildly. Talbot and I cleared customs quickly though, and then were met by very friendly officials. In a few hours we were comfortably ensconced in the Hotel Indonesia in Djakarta.

Saturday, August 5, 1967, 10 P.M.

We are on board the motor ship *Samudera*, a 200-ton diesel

The Indian rhinoceros photographed at Kazingaranga, Assam, in 1968 has only one horn.

vessel belonging to the Marine Research Department of the National Biological Institute of Indonesia. We left Djakarta about midnight today, or maybe it was still August 4—but this is trivial after five incredible days of Southeast Asian diplomacy in the capital. Three different groups have been wrestling for control of the country's science programs, including conservation, and Talbot, who knows them all, steered me from one contact to another, keeping each one happy.

Our being on the *Samudera* is not entirely by choice. A letter from Charles A. Lindbergh to Sultan Buwono, the third-ranking cabinet minister in the government, had stirred up great activity in Djakarta in anticipation of *Life's* visit. At my first meeting with Dr. Suhadi, head of the country's science programs, I was surprised to discover that his department had made an elaborate plan for my coverage of Udjong Kulon. To begin with, I was to use the *Samudera* as a base camp offshore. Next, six Indonesian scientists—the departments of biology, zoology, marine biology, forestry, and game were all represented—had been chosen to help me do my story. In addition, the government's official tourist agency, Nitour, had appointed a safari

The 200-ton vessel Samudera *took the expedition from Djakarta to Udjong Kulon.*

manager, Mr. Sugiyono, to provide every possible comfort for the expedition, and Mr. Sugiyono, I learned, had hired a chef and two assistants from the Hotel Indonesia in Djakarta.

The *Samudera* was to cost $250 U.S. per day, running or not, and the safari $25 a day per man. For a two-month stay in Java the cost would be about $30,000.

After my shocked reaction Dr. Suhadi brought out a $10,000 figure based on a shorter stay and a smaller group. I will not forget how we sat around a coffee table at the side of his office; the doctor had just explained how he had been a very efficient cabinet minister under Sukarno—I believe there were more than fifty ministers then—and told us that he was a good manager and that the plan for our expedition was all set. I tried to explain that I could not take even two scientists with me, that Dr. Talbot was going to be with me only for a week or ten days in the sanctuary, just to acquaint me with it, and that after that it was almost a solitary job. Groups can't operate well in the isolation of a jungle. Too many people and temperaments to take care of, too much distraction, and too much noise.

Finally, this got through to the good doctor, who then turned us over to a division of his, the Forestry Department. That afternoon Talbot and I drove south from Djakarta to the lovely hill town of Bogor, where Forestry had its headquarters. There we met with Dr. Sudjarwo, its director-general, and Dr. Basjarudin, its director. The head of conservation, Made Taman, was in Germany recovering from an eye operation, or he would have been our key contact. By the end of the conference we managed to convince the Forestry Department officials that we didn't need the *Samudera*; we'd hire a small fishing boat at Labuan, a seaport near the sanctuary, and use that for logistical support.

Talbot had worked with Wolman Sinaga, a senior game warden, in 1964, and we made a formal request for Sinaga to become the representative of the department on the *Life* expedition, which was granted. Since Sinaga spoke adequate English, the rest of the personnel could be ordinary Sundanese people from a village near the sanctuary. Talbot and I estimated that we'd need about eight men: a camp manager and a cook, who would stay in base headquarters once it was established, two more men, preferably with experience in the Game Department, who knew the animals and could track them, and about four men to carry the cameras and camping equipment on the many sorties we'd have to make to cover the various parts of the sanctuary. All this was agreed to in the presence of Sugiyono, the safari man, who became sadder and sadder as the prospects of his becoming a Nairobi type dimmed out altogether.

The upshot was that we were to get a boat for about $25 a day, as against $250, and could support our eight-man crew at about $1 a day each for food and about $10 a week each in salary, as against the $25 a day each it would have cost for the scientists' upkeep plus salaries. (Most Indonesian government officials have second jobs, since the pay scale is so low that it is impossible to live on just one salary.)

I chartered the *Samudera* to bring us to Udjong Kulon as a

small face-saving gesture. It had been standing by for us—or so, anyway, I was told—and I thought it would be polite to at least allow the Marine Research Department to earn $500 for the two days it's supposed to take the *Samudera* to get us to Udjong Kulon and itself back to port. I wasn't sure of the two days and asked if we could pay by the hour after the first day, but I was told $250 per day or any part of one. This made me very nervous, since I can't control the voyage back, and the ship might break down, run aground, or boondoggle up a huge bill. Finally I said $500 for the whole trip, or no *Samudera*. The offer, made while we were still in Bogor, was accepted.

We left Bogor in good spirits, having ordered the *Samudera* to be ready on August 4. This gave us a day before sailing to buy food for the expedition. It must be remembered that once we left Djakarta, we left behind all adequate sources for provisions. There is an international food and appliance store in Djakarta where all purchases are made in U.S. dollars. Diplomats and press people do not pay local tax. I stocked up on what I thought might be needed for at least two months in the jungle, and this filled ten large cartons.

The *Samudera* was supposed to sail at about 5 P.M. yesterday, but the captain had not obtained the proper clearances to leave Djakarta when we arrived at the port, and since yesterday was a Friday, a Moslem holy day, the port officials could not be found. We were told to wait until Monday, for all offices were closed over the weekend. But with us to cope with problems like this was Sri Budojo, an assistant of Sultan Buwono. Sri Budojo can only be described as a real operator; he could fix anything. It took him five hours, but he found the captain of the port and another functionary whose signature was necessary—and off we sailed.

To our surprise, we discovered Mr. Sugiyono, the safari man, on board the *Samudera,* with a photographer from the Forestry Department as well. Both carried full camping gear. I know the sanctuary is more theirs than ours. But I wasn't going to have someone camping near us. Sugiyono claimed he'd leave in a week, but couldn't produce on what boat.

I didn't want amateurs in the area I was going to work in I told him, and after explaining—at length—I convinced him, then the Forestry man, to go back on the *Samudera* when she returned.

The *Samudera* stopped at Labuan in the morning, a small seaport four hours west of Djakarta by car, and here with the help of Mr. Djuhari, the game warden in charge of Udjong Kulon, we found the *Harini*—the name means "today" in Indonesian—and made a quick deal with the owner's agent, Ong Tjibun, a Chinese Indonesian, to charter her and crew. The

Sailboats are anchored in the river that empties into the sea at Labuan.

24

Harini is to follow us to Udjong Kulon.

At Labuan we also bought a large dugout canoe to use in ship-to-shore operations, and we hired and took on board the *Samudera* Amir Hasan, a young, educated clerk in the Forestry office at Labuan, who speaks a little English. Amir will be our camp manager.

Our next stop was at Tamandjaja, the nearest village of farmers and fishermen, on the north shore of the western end of Java, just before the neck of land which opens up into the Udjong Kulon sanctuary. We went ashore in the ship's boat and chose the men who'll be picked up by the *Harini* tomorrow. While on shore, I bought a dozen chickens, a small goat, and a pair of Muscovy ducks.

The *Harini* isn't a fishing boat; it makes its living running freight and passengers from Labuan to Tamandjaja and points in between—there are no roads west of Labuan, so all transport is by sea. I asked Ong Tjinbun, the agent, to procure fishing gear and put it aboard the *Harini,* since I expect the sea to be our main source of fresh food. Feeding the crew isn't going to be a problem. They eat rice three times a day, augmented by noodles, peanuts, beans, and any vegetables they can get, like cabbage, onions, or carrots, and finally either fresh fish or dry salted varieties. Fish about the size of an index finger can be smelled and seen drying on the beaches of every fishing town of Java and are the country's major protein.

The Harini, *a thirty-foot launch powered by a 1952 Dodge truck engine, was chartered by the author.*

*Small fish are dri(
the sun at Taman(
the nearest village
Udjong Kulon.*

In Djakarta I'd bought plenty of canned corn beef, Spam, and frankfurters, pork and beans and chili, tuna fish and sardines and tomato herring, fruit and juices of all kinds, and such canned vegetables as beets, string beans, and asparagus, which are excellent as salad. I also bought olive oil, vinegar, and garlic, as well as jars of mayonnaise. I didn't forget powdered milk and Quick Quaker Oats; this, cooked together, makes a good breakfast to start any hard working day. I have brown sugar and honey for sweetening. There are canned butter, peanut butter, jam, and cheese from Australia. I also bought packages of egg noodles and spaghetti, since I expect I'll get tired of rice. Funke's canned pumpernickel (from Holland) may prove invaluable, for the Indonesians are not bread bakers (the safari cooks in East Africa make great bread every day on the campfire); I also have several boxes of Bisquick and might try that if desperate. Of course there's tea and coffee, and there's Rose's Lime Juice and other flavors for the boiled water—flavors like bourbon and Scotch. I even have a case of wine, since I believe nothing is too good for the working class.

The fact that I had picked up a kerosene refrigerator en route to Djakarta encouraged me to buy perishable items like fresh eggs and vegetables in Labuan. I also bought a dozen bottles of local beer, for which I was grateful at dinner. The *Samudera's* spicy food is typically Indonesian—or rather, has been since we convinced the captain that we're prepared to eat the same as the crew. He once had a Japanese TV group on board who refused to, and he was avoiding a conflict with us, or so he thought. This afternoon I noticed the cook very carefully weigh the meat for the crew's meal, and actually snip off about a two-ounce piece as too much! I'm not about to try to break into our own stores, below decks; anyway—and I made this clear to the captain—at $250 a day he can jolly well feed us plentifully. Dinner was fine, and all in all, the trip on the *Samudera* has been fairly pleasant.

Talbot and I each have a small cabin—one bunk, a sink, and a porthole. Last night I discovered the sheet is too short for the bunk. It kept crawling up, which is annoying anywhere. Talbot was annoyed by this too. He was also upset because the *Samudera* had been fitted out as a marine research vessel by the World Wildlife Fund, and the laboratory on board has somehow disappeared.

The *Samudera* is now anchored for the night—it will be our second on board—in the bay off Tamandjaja, since the captain is in no great hurry and our route will be easier by daylight. Also, Talbot and I feel it will be advantageous if he can point out some of the physical characteristics of the sanctuary as we steam by.

We left Tamandjaja at six this morning, and the long peninsula stretched out before us. A narrow sandy beach, a few yards of heavy beach foliage or bushes and low trees, and rising up from these, bank and bank of dense foliage—the top of a rain forest (average rainfall in Udjong Kulon is 125 inches a year) varying only in its light to dark greens, undulating upward, interrupted by spaces seen only by the change of sharpness as the hills march farther and farther away, going up and down toward the backbone of the peninsula. A few shore birds, not even one exotic, were dotted here and there against the green wall. Of the rich animal life Udjong Kulon is famous for, not a specimen was to be seen from the *Samudera.*

We finally anchored at midday between Peutjang island and the mainland opposite, once the site of a village named Djung Kulon, which was destroyed by a tidal wave from the eruption of Krakatau in 1883. The watchtower on the mainland, built here by the Game Department, is between two rivers, the Tjidaon and the Tjidjung Kulon. *Tji* means river and *daon* is leaves; *djung kulon* means western tip.

The kerosene refrigerator picked up in Singapore is carefully brought ashore from the Samudera.

We unloaded our gear from the *Samudera,* placing it in the long boat, which we beached near the shore. The water was too

29

low for us to reach dry land. It took four men to carry the kerosene refrigerator from the long boat to the tower.

A Swiss scientist, Rudolf Schenkel, and his wife, Lotte, are living on Peutjang island, in quarters built by the Game Department for their personnel. The Schenkels have a grant from the World Wildlife Fund to study rhinoceros behavior, and they've been on Peutjang for several months. He is an animal behavior man from Basle University, and since the almost extinct Java rhinoceros is my principal target in the sanctuary, I have hopes of help from him. Mrs. Schenkel is a medical doctor, and this, too, is reassuring, although I carry a very complete medical kit and fancy myself a fair first-aid man.

Dr. Schenkel is about fifty years old, small, wiry, and balding, with a fringe of grayish hair around his head; his eager bright blue eyes sparkle with excitement. Mrs. Schenkel is a sturdy, substantial woman of about forty. She's perhaps a bit taller than her husband, and quite attractive.

The Schenkels, to whom Talbot introduced me this afternoon, were worried that we might want to use their second building. It's only a few yards from the one they live in and houses two of their staff (from Bogor's Game Department).

All water-crossings were made with the cameras in a water-proof sack lashed to an inflated scooter tire

But I want privacy just as much as the Schenkels do. I also have no intention of isolating myself on an island and having to cross a deep channel to the mainland every time I work there. More photography expeditions have come to grief crossing water than perhaps any other way. Doing it in a tippy dugout canoe would compound the problem. I'm willing to do it when necessary, but first, I always make provisions to safeguard the equipment. My camera cases are fitted into large waterproof sacks that can be lashed to inflated scooter tires; thus if my canoe upsets, the equipment will float bone dry to shore. When I discovered that the Schenkels had managed to turn over twice, ruining most of their camera gear, I was rather superior about it all.

The game observation tower mentioned by Lindbergh in his letter, built less than ten years ago, is well on its way to extinction, since no one has kept it up. Some of the tiles on the roof are gone; so are half the windows. Tomorrow our men can plait arenga palm fronds, which will make adequate window shades, and construct a new roof of palm underneath the old one.

The tower is a fair-sized hut on top of a twenty-foot structure, and excellent for several reasons. Most important, it's right on the edge of a large grazing ground to which many animals come. It should be easy to keep clean, and if necessary, it can be locked up. Also, it's above the trees, where it will catch every cool breeze at night.

Of the two rivers the tower is between, only one, the Tjidaon, isn't salty. This will be our source of water—boiled, of course. In Djakarta I purchased two large earthenware jugs in which to cool and store the water after boiling.

When I first climbed into the tower I saw from one of the windows some bantengs, wild animals closely resembling dairy cattle, and from another window, peacocks. I watched the animals for a while—and found I could do fairly close shots of any of them with a 1000mm mirror lens. This is a Nikon lens of F11 aperture, and it does not have an iris diaphragm. You shoot at F11. Since it is better to move the mirror of a reflex camera up and out of the way when using a 20X magnification lens— in order to avoid vibration—I found it unsatisfactory as an animal lens; by the time you focus and frame your picture there is no time to move the mirror, because the animal or bird has also moved. I took my chances at having the mirror move with the exposure, and it resulted in many of my 1000mm pictures being slightly unsharp. This isn't always important. In fact, lack of sharpness has often contributed to the beauty of a particular photograph. Like that of an actress. But pigs and deer are not movie stars, and their detail is of interest. One cannot make a hard-and-fast rule about this. Each subject and picture is different. I also have a 500mm Nikon mirror lens, an F5, which is high speed, and expect to use that one a good deal. It might be of interest to list the lenses I brought with me to Udjong Kulon, for my four Nikon F (reflex 35mm) cameras.

21mm F4
28mm F3.5
35mm F2.8
Short 42mm–86mm zoom F3.5
55mm Micro-Nikkor for close-ups
58mm F1.4
105mm F2.5
200mm F4
300mm F4.5
500mm F5
1000mm F11

The lenses I usually find most useful are the 28mm, short zoom, and 200mm. These I have in a small camera bag with two of the cameras, a Weston exposure meter, and a bunch of film. The rest are in another bag, to be carried by one of the trackers.

I have several hundred rolls of film, mostly Kodachrome II and some high-speed Ektachrome; most of this is stored in the refrigerator until needed. But you can't use film that's just come out of the cold, because moisture condenses on its surface; you must wait after four hours to be safe. More important, exposed color film must be kept cool until developed.

I have two tripods, both Quickset: a light one for portability

Banteng cow and calf photographed with a 1000mm mirror lens from a tower window.

The author standing in front of the game observation tower, which became expedition headquarters.

and a heavy one for stationary setups, like the tower window. I also have two small strobe lights for interiors, balancing hard sunlight outdoors on close-ups, and the like. I brought two Weston meters and two Lunasix ones as well, and a Pentax spot meter. I also have a small underwater outfit: the Nikonos camera designed by Cousteau and a Sekonic underwater exposure meter. And I brought twenty-four cans of silica gel to dry the moisture out of my cameras and lenses. I don't have a developing outfit with me to make tests, but I'll be able to determine exposure meter accuracy by trial shooting with the roll film Polaroid camera I did bring with me. I have one more camera, a 35mm Widelux, a panorama camera with a view of 140 degrees. I also have a tele-extender, which doubles the focal length of any telephoto lens.

Tuesday, August 8

After spending most of yesterday, our first full day, getting settled in the tower and selecting a place on the river for getting water, a good distance upstream from bathing facilities, Talbot and I discussed our game survey of Udjong Kulon. The last one was conducted by Talbot in 1964, and he is very keen to see if there have been any significant changes in the animal population since then. Five teams were organized, each led by a warden from the Game Department.

The interior of tower headquarters showing improvised furniture and the author using mirror lenses.

Most of the groups consist of three men. Talbot's and mine is considerably larger, since we're carrying camping gear and most of my camera equipment. We're also going to take the longest, since Talbot has assigned our group to cut right across the center of the sanctuary from east to west. The five teams have been so placed that all will transverse the sanctuary on somewhat parallel routes, depending upon terrain, in order to obtain the widest possible survey of the animal life on the peninsula.

The teams have been instructed by Talbot to record every sign of animal life: actual specimens, footprints, feces, and affected vegetation (for example, a bush eaten or knocked down by a rhinoceros). As in all surveys, not every animal will be encountered, but some general idea of population can be formed.

I'm not very happy about starting my stay on Udjong Kulon by walking and climbing for five or more days across its middle, up and down hills and ravines. The sanctuary rises to about 1,600 feet near its western end. Fortunately we're not scheduled to include this terrain in our survey.

I'd hardly become accustomed to the over 100° temperature before, early this morning, Talbot had us all on the *Harini*—it arrived yesterday—for the various drops offshore. We wished each team good luck. Two of them are carrying well-rusted rifles, which I think are emotional security rather than actual.

Our team consists of Talbot as leader, Wolman Sinaga, the game warden who is to stay with me after Talbot leaves, Harum and Enang, two first-class animal trackers, normally farmers from the Tamandjaja region, four porters, and Sohib, a so-called cook. Amir, the camp manager, is staying at the tower as guardian, since we're leaving lots of gear and food behind.

Talbot brought plastic rulers with him and has distributed them to the teams so they can measure the exact size of any rhino footprints they find. This is crucial, since although the prints will all be about eight inches across, each animal is different enough to make it possible to identify different rhinos by the exact size of their prints. Rhino prints can usually be found only in the mud at the edges of rivers and streams. There are plenty of rivers and streams in the sanctuary but because it's now the dry season, most of them will be dry, especially in the highlands of the peninsula. Talbot has also given each group leader mimeographed sheets (he prepared these in Washington to make notations on), and a small pocket flashlight. Untypically for a scientist, he didn't forget to be thoughtful to the men, bringing lipsticks for the wardens he's worked with before to give their wives and binoculars (he and I bought these at the airport in Singapore) as gifts for the three senior men. The typical scientist's one-degree field of view of the world is likely to comprehend little more than the activities of, say, a particular species of wasp; Talbot appreciates many things besides wild-life ecology, the field in which he's outstanding.

I'm looking forward to the survey with some misgivings. I said this before—with reason. To begin with, I'm not an athlete, nor am I in constant training. For a man in his middle fifties I'm in very good condition, since I don't smoke, drink only moderately, and keep my weight at a comfortable bulge— but not anywhere in proportion to my interest in and appetite for good food. I do some walking in New York, trying to go to the Time-Life Building in Rockefeller Center from my apart-ment on East 27th Street at least one way each day; it's little over a mile, but made at good speed to achieve exercise. I don't go to a gymnasium, nor do I play golf. When I'm in my summer home in Maine, I do cut some firewood, swim, row a small boat, and sail, but this can hardly be called keeping in condition. So when Talbot set up the march by compass across the heart of the sanctuary, up and down every hill and ravine we're going to come to, I didn't lick my lips in anticipation. I'd have much preferred to wait a week, doing daily marches or even two-day sorties on easier terrain for starters. But Talbot's eager to do the survey and has the men with him for the purpose. Since he's leaving in just ten days, I couldn't veto the plan. Talbot also argued that this survey will serve to immediately assess which animals are where, and after all, finding animals—par-ticularly the rhino—is what I'm here for.

I've lived through some fairly uncomfortable expeditions in Africa and New Guinea; this one probably won't be worse. Being blessed with a really strong constitution, I was a good athlete as a youth; I'm still well coordinated, and even more important in the bush, I still have remarkably fast reflexes. But I'm not happy.

We're traveling light, since this is a reconnaissance. The beautiful roomy nine-by-twelve-foot tent with sewn-in floor and big screened windows on all sides has been left behind. Our porters will have enough to carry with just bedding, food, and camera equipment. The survey will, if our estimates are correct, take four to six days.

I brought two air mattresses, sleeping bags, and mosquito nets to Java. One of the nets was for Talbot, but Talbot had brought his own. I also brought three large waterproof nylon tarpaulins, two of which I have with me now. One is to suspend at an angle over our heads—from four trees—and the other to use as a ground cloth. The men will make their own shelter from palm fronds, which they'll cut and use to build an overhead roof and a floor to sleep on. We could do the same, but that would leave us the problem of sheltering the equipment: the cameras are in two Halliburton aluminum shower- and dust-proof cases, but are not totally secure.

The *Harini* was to leave with the five teams just after dawn, but we didn't get off until almost 9 A.M. Too many people to get together from where they were staying, some at a camp near us and others at Dr. Schenkel's headquarters on Peutjang island. Talbot held a briefing for these men, with Sinaga translating, under the shelter of a tarpaulin rigged midship on the *Harini*. The sun here near the equator is extremely hot, with the temperature going to 120° F., but it falls to about 80° in the shade, and the movement of the *Harini*—about five knots an hour is my guess—helps a lot.

It's now nearly noon, and we've dropped off three of the teams opposite the shores they are to start from. Two of these are the teams with rifles—and one look at the rusty barrels convinced me that we're lucky not to have one. Our only weapon is a Walther .765 automatic pistol, the gun James Bond made famous; I've had it since World War II, when I was a war correspondent and needed a back pocket gun. Every time I see guns in the hands of people I don't know, I worry. Once, in the late

Dr. Talbot, with Sinaga at his right, briefing survey team leaders on the deck of the Harini.

forties, I had to photograph Angkor, the great complex of temples in Cambodia—and there was a civil war on. Forty Cambodians under a French noncommissioned officer formed a cordon around each temple I worked in, but my greatest danger was from the accidental discharge of old rifles; one bullet chipped off a bit of low-relief carving near me.

The prospect of a jungle march and the thought of the rifles also recalls one of my worst experiences in thirty years of photojournalism, an episode that almost ended my life. This was in 1951, in Gabon, which was then part of French Equatorial Africa. I had already climbed and photographed the Ruwenzori, which Stanley took to be the fabled "Mountains of the Moon." The range, between the Congo and Uganda, is one of the starting places of the Albert Nile. The experience I'm thinking of took place on an expedition to capture live young gorillas for psychological experiments at Yale University. I can't describe it in detail here. We were three Europeans, William Said, an American, myself, and 107 Africans, and we reached the gorilla area by driving Dodge power wagons for several days through grasslands and bush, making our own ferries across

A game warden carries his rifle when one of the teams goes ashore to start the survey.

rivers and so on. When the scouts found a gorilla family with young ones, we had to keep after it on foot—through some of the worst swamps and low forest I ever encountered. I spent several days wading through mud, sleeping on an air mattress laid over twigs on soggy ground. And since no one was available to supervise the daily boiling of river water, drinking—at least I drank it once, which was enough—what turned out to be infested water. The result was that I developed a violent case of dysentery, which later, when I finally reached Brazzaville in one of the power wagons, was diagnosed as amoebic. My antibiotic having had almost no effect on the disease, I lost fifteen pounds in four days and spent two weeks recovering enough to work again.

But that was later. Before that, the mature gorillas had had to be killed to capture the young ones, which was horrible. The head of the family, who weighed about six hundred pounds, did his best to lead his family through our cordon. But the Africans had cleared a circle around the group of trees that was the animal's last stand, then hung nets made of strong vines to completely cut off the animals' escape.

Our group had large-caliber rifles. In addition, I had a twelve-gauge pump gun loaded with buckshot. The gun was held upright by an African whose elbow rested against me to show he was there; whenever the pressure was gone I looked for the gun. I also had a .45 Colt automatic in a shoulder holster. The Africans had ancient muzzle-loading guns, charged with gunpowder and pieces of metal. The one that almost cut the male gorilla in half had a wooden stick topped with a sharp iron half-moon placed in the barrel and was fired at close range.

The only pleasant thing that happened to me on the whole expedition happened early, before we started tracking the gorillas. I insisted the members of the group try their weapons. The leader, William Said (who died before he was thirty, in Africa), and the other three Europeans were great with their Mannlichers and Remingtons. Then they looked at my Colt .45. Normally I couldn't hit a barn with it. Now there was nothing I could do but draw down on the cardboard carton fifty feet away and fire as it crossed the target. I'd never been able to hold this gun steady. Yet to my utter amazement, I almost centered the shot. Although each of the other men had fired a clip of five or six cartridges, I knew when I was well off and holstered my gun as if one shot was enough. My reputation as a sharpshooter had been made. But enough of that. I won't even mention that my shirt was torn off by a half-grown gorilla in close combat, or that the upper arm of a baby gorilla was broken. I set the arm with cotton-wrapped tongue depressors, and saw that the baby was carried in a specially woven openwork basket so the arm could heal. I must also forget the night that safari ants—or army ants, as they're sometimes called—marched toward our camp. These ants eat everything in their path—which this time would have been three caged gorillas. We stopped—or rather, barely detoured—these unbelievable insects by hastily digging a ditch around the camp, filling the ditch with diesel oil and kerosene, then setting it on fire.

The close quarters of the *Harini*—it is under thirty feet long—have given me a chance to really study our team. Indonesians are smaller than we are, are light brown or tan in complexion, and have heavy, straight black hair and black eyes with the typical Oriental eyefold. Although they're very clean in their habits, the men—our men anyway—wear tattered clothing that makes them look like derelicts. Several have singlets, cotton undershirts without sleeves, that are more holes than cloth.

All the men are friendly enough, but as in every group, one man seems to be somewhat of a clown. Sanara, who's wearing a small black Moslem cap, has already displayed a whole repertoire of doleful expressions, in which his eyes are fully used. He has the strongest pair of legs and will probably carry the heaviest

The dugout canoe, too heavy to tow, is dragged aboard the Harini *after landing each team.*

loads. Another porter, Suleman, is wearing a sharp white European-style Panama hat. I'd have liked to ask him to leave the hat behind; it's out of character for him, but worse than that, being bright white, it's always going to be overexposed in pictures made in the forest. I didn't ask though, because I couldn't bear to intrude on Suleman's privacy, or to upset his pride in owning such a wonderful hat. [Suleman had his trouser legs rolled down at this point; otherwise I'd have seen some extraordinary scars and still active infections—caused by the kind of small ticks that were going to devil our survey.] Another porter, Kiflie, is a bit on the skinny side and doesn't look too healthy to me. [As it turned out, after the survey he was almost incapable of any work, and he finally had to be sent home on the *Harini*.] The fourth porter is Kadir, who seems rather phlegmatic, with no particularly distinguishing traits.

The two animal trackers, Harum and Enang, are both characters. Harum is rather tall, good-looking, and slightly arrogant, or at least superior in his posture and attitude. Enang is sweet and friendly.

Our cook, Sohib, is, like Harum and Enang, a farmer from Tamandjaja, but he's about ten years older, and considerably less experienced at what will be his chore. Having done it for the Game Department, he knows about campfire Indonesian cooking—whatever that is. Since his principal job is to cook for our men, this is okay. Because cooking is my best hobby, if not more important than that, no one's apt to stop me from doing

Talbot is first of his team to go ashore at the mouth of the Tjigenter.

part of the survey's cooking. I suspect some of my style may rub off on Sohib.

The *Harini* has reached the mouth of the Tjigenter, the largest river in the sanctuary, and our team is preparing to disembark opposite Handeuleum island (on which the Game Department maintains a warden and his family in a stone house). First, some of the camping material and food will be lowered over the side into the dugout canoe. My camera cases are in the deckhouse, being placed into large waterproof sacks; the sacks will be firmly knotted to prevent any water from entering, and then they'll be lashed to two fully inflated scooter tires, which will keep the equipment afloat in the event of mishap.

We've arranged for the *Harini* to wait forty-eight hours at this spot, anchored of course, then to proceed back to her normal anchorage in the channel between Peutjang island and the beach adjoining the Tjidaon tower, our headquarters. The reason for waiting is to ensure a means of return if someone is hurt. When the two days are up, we'll presumably have passed the point of no return, and like the usual movie airplane with engine trouble, we'll just have to push on.

Sunday, August 13, 8 A.M.

We are back at headquarters after five days of marching, and I am in the Tjidaon tower writing on a nice table made from the plywood case that housed our kerosene refrigerator from Sweden to Singapore to Udjong Kulon. My very first action when we reached the tower yesterday was to open the refrigerator—it has a lock—and take out two large cold bottles of Indonesian beer. Talbot and I slowly sipped it down. It tasted like the greatest drink in the world. The Heineken people taught the Indonesians to make beer during Dutch rule, and it is excellent. That first drink after five days of boiled water and liana juice was just too much. I felt sorry I hadn't bought more than a dozen bottles [but the beer never tasted as good again].

I'm tired but in good shape. The human body sometimes amazes me. On the whole trip I was never too exhausted to continue walking. I carried only one small camera bag, which helped; the leather bag contained a Nikon F loaded with Kodachrome II, with 28mm, short zoom, and 200mm lenses, about ten rolls of Kodachrome II and high-speed Ektachrome, a Weston meter, and also, in the front pocket, a suction-cup snakebite outfit. I had the other Nikon around my neck, loaded with high-speed Ektachrome, usually with the 105mm F2.5 lens. This was double the normal focal length, magnifying the image twice as large, and yet not so long that I couldn't keep it steady hand held at a slow shutter speed. Once we entered the forest, Kodachrome was useless except on a tripod with stationary subjects, like trees. My only hope of catching an animal en route was to be able to whip up the camera and shoot almost instantly. To this end, I kept adjusting the shutter and aperture settings as the locale and time of day changed the intensity of light. Many times I shot and didn't know if I'd gotten away with it.

Our survey team [as you can see from the map on the end papers] crossed the peninsula from opposite Handeuleum island and went westward and then southwest for about two-thirds of the way, then changed to northwest to reach the tower. This was all done on pure compass direction, since there were no landmarks or trails to follow. A major problem was how far we had gone. Checking my altimeter with the height—shown on our large-scale map—of various hills we crossed gave us some orientation. But difficulties were caused by the map, which turned out to be very inaccurate, especially in the placement of rivers. Often a river was indicated, but we found none; of those we did find almost all were dry, waiting for the rains to come to activate them once more. The dry river beds had cut shallow ravines in the forest floor; most still had some mud in places. The Tjigenter, the mouth of which was our starting point, kept crisscrossing over our due-west route and became a terrible nuisance.

On the very first day, I suffered a small embarrassment with the group. Most of the men had walked across the Tjigenter on a dead tree that had fallen lengthwise over the river's bed. I followed, proceeded a few wobbly feet, then suddenly thought, what if I fall off and break a leg? I had two Nikons to protect, and because I lost my nerve, I used them as an excuse for sitting down on the log when I was partially across. Without much shame I sat down and shimmied my bottom across. Ignominious, but practical.

We didn't get very far the first day, since we didn't start till midafternoon. It was good to let my muscles out a bit. Talbot's just as tough as the Indonesians, but I'm not.

Our walking order consisted of Harum as lead man, then Talbot, then Enang and me, followed by the rest of the men; Sinaga was usually at the end, keeping the column together. Enang had the larger Nikon Halliburton case, which resembles a one-suiter, strapped to a metal-frame pack carrier I had brought with me for that purpose.

The first man and sometimes Talbot did the chopping. Without the machete going all the time there was no way to get through this jungle. Udjong Kulon is a typical low-lying tropical rain forest, with dense foliage, all of it primary (but most of the really original flora was swept away by the Krakatau tidal wave). No one has cut it. This foliage consists of large trees, smaller ones, bushes, and many varieties of vine and rattan.

The vines vary from finger thickness to that of a man's thigh; the rattans come in innumerable species, all of which are equipped with murderous thorns and barbs—not simple thorns, but bent ones, curved like fishhooks and placed most thickly not on the trunk of the plant, but on long whiplike ribs extending from the end of each leaf. The rattan actually climbs to the sun as the fronds catch successively higher branches and keep growing upward out of the deep forest shade. The barbed tips are very delicate and sway gently in the wind; unless severed by the lead men, they think nothing of catching on your face or neck and tearing out a piece. When one hooks you, you stop dead, then backtrack and try to disengage the barb. Doing this all day is no pleasure. Some of the other plants had thorns, but they were nothing compared with the rattans.

Once we left the flat land of the narrow coastal belt, we began going up and down. The ups and downs were never so abrupt that what we did could be called climbing, but they were steep enough—especially since the ground was made very slippery by millions of decaying leaves. The age-old habit of grabbing a tree branch or bush to hang on to was quickly cured with the

Bright green whip snake is small but has poisonous rear fangs to kill its prey.

first thorns. It seems that everything that grows here has sharp defenses.

There are several species of poisonous snakes in the sanctuary, but they are rarely seen. The noise of a group of men cutting through the jungle is enough to scare them away. There are very few snakes in the world that will attack unless they are disturbed. The black mamba in Africa will come at you, so will the

group uses a n tree to cross the st dry Tjigenter.

45

Australian taipan, but you have to step on—or almost on—most snakes before they will strike at you.

When people ask me about my trips one of the first questions is usually about insects. I suppose we're just lucky it's still the dry season. There are practically no mosquitoes. Which doesn't mean I'm not taking antimalaria pills, to be swallowed faithfully every six days—two pills each time, because all the combination pills-in-one are going to Vietnam.

I was bitten a few times during the survey, but considerably less often than I'd have been bitten in Maine. By mosquitoes, that is. Ticks were another matter entirely. These small insects —when swollen with blood they're about the size of a pea— fall on you as you go through the forest, puncture your skin, and imbed their heads in the flesh beneath. By a unique arrangement of hooks on their heads, once these miserable creatures are imbedded, they stay imbedded. But they're not content to dig in just anywhere. Indeed, they crawl over your body until they find a cozy spot. I even took one off my scrotal sac.

Talbot has a nice way of caring for ticks. He uses steel tweezers, and by both twisting and pulling as he grabs the tick,

Talbot and the author slept in mosquito nets slung under a nylon tarpaulin.

he usually gets all of the creature out. The danger is that part of the tick may break off, leaving the head still in your flesh where, more often than not, it causes a minor infection. Later I found a better method. I had a spray bottle of ethyl chloride, which doctors use to anesthetize small areas of skin during minor surgery. I had this with me as a tranquilizer for small reptiles and insects I didn't want to kill but did want to slow down for photography. I discovered that a spritz of this stuff made the tick release its head; whereupon a straight pull with the tweezers took care of the whole little beast. All the men are covered with scars from old tick infections, and sores from new ones. They scratch these all the time, with very dirty fingernails.

Tuesday night we made our first camp, about two kilometers, a little less than a mile, from where we'd started out. We were near a dry river bed, which we hoped would yield enough water to cook our dinner. It didn't, but in less than half an hour all the men who'd gone out scouting for water came back with armfuls of heavy vines. These vines are as thick as your arm; rooted in the ground, they climb a hundred or more feet up the trees to reach the sun. Water goes from the ground to the top, and the

A four-foot length of vine provides about a half-pint of sweet water.

entire length of vine is loaded with it. The water has just a trace of sweet taste to it. By cutting short, pointed lengths of vine, the water can be made to drip out at an even rate. One gets about a half pint of water from about four feet or so of vine. We drank by holding the vines over our open mouths, the way Spaniards hold their wine jugs, but I didn't find this too easy. Some of the vine water—or juice—we used to boil our rice for dinner. The only water we carried on the survey was in two small canteens I had with me, and I usually filled one with tea. This improved the taste of river water that had been boiled, or if not boiled, doctored with Halazone water purifier tablets.

The men also cut many fronds of arenga palm, the single most useful plant in Udjong Kulon. Arenga palm is called *langkap* in Sundanese, the language and people of West Java, but game wardens have learned its Latin name, *Arenga*; its full name is *Arenga obtusifolium*. It has large leaves, like the coconut, and most important, no thorns. This makes it easy to handle. The men brought in dozens of branches and spread them out to sleep on. I thought they'd weave some of the leaves together to make a roof, but because it's the dry season, a roof wasn't necessary. Each man slept in a cotton blanket of some sort, in which he completely wrapped himself, covering even his head. I was shocked the next morning to see what looked like a row of mummies near the fire, which had been kept going during the night. Plenty of wood had been found near our campsite and cut up with a "golok," the Indonesian machete. Everybody carries one, and it is used as a knife as well as an ax.

I'd been too busy the first day just putting my feet up and down and not falling on my face to take many pictures or observe very much. I think Talbot was slightly relieved to find that I wasn't holding the group back with interminable stops for painstaking photography. Not that I wouldn't have stopped, since for me, photography was what the whole thing was about. But I don't believe in photographing everything in sight. In a situation like this—a march of four or five days across unknown terrain—you do photograph anything of interest. You never know if there's a better shot five minutes or five hours farther on, but you do know that it's easy to discard a first picture in favor of a second—and impossible to go back to photograph something you missed. Even so, I exposed fewer than five rolls of color film, thirty-six frames to the roll, that second day.

Like any professional photographer, I bracket my exposures. This means that if your meter indicates an exposure of 1/60 at F11, you shoot at this, then shoot several other frames with more and less exposure. That way you're sure to get the one or two best shots. In the forest of Udjong Kulon brackets aren't really enough. Since the tree cover overhead is not a continuous umbrella, patches of bright sunlight spatter the intense gloom underneath. It was impossible to expose for both sun and shade, and I had constantly to decide what I was concentrating on. The best practice was to avoid contrasty subjects, but this wasn't always possible.

We began the second day with a new compass bearing west

10 degrees south, and were still crisscrossing the Tjigenter. We didn't leave camp until 8:30 A.M.—late because it was our first breaking of camp and loading of gear. In the following days this became routine, each man finding his chores to do. Enang turned out to be invaluable. He caught on to our needs as quickly as they became apparent. After the first night he knew how I wanted the tarpaulin hung and to blow up the air mattresses. I never allowed him or the others to hang my mosquito net. Not that the net was sacred, but its suspension underneath the tarp took some judgment—about where to tie it on, how much slack to leave in the cords, on which side provision would be made to crawl under, and so on. Most important, the bottom of the net had to be tucked in carefully under the air mattress to make a seal against insects and snakes. The net is rather narrow, cot width, so I couldn't help thinking how easy it would be for a snake to strike me at the place where my body touched the net; for that matter, a mosquito could quite easily poke its beak through and suck blood to its heart's content.

Talbot measures a rhinoceros footprint in the mud at the edge of the Tjigenter near a group of arenga palms.

Wednesday morning, about an hour after we started out, Talbot, who has eyes like an eagle—nothing escapes him—spotted a fresh rhino track in one of the still wet portions of the Tjigenter. Here was my first encounter with the "badak," as Indonesians call the rhinoceros. The print looked like a small

49

dinner plate with three Ping-Pong balls pressed down above it. Talbot measured the print carefully and noted the measurements. Since the dry forest floor nearby didn't show any more prints, there was nothing to follow. We couldn't have tracked the badak anyway, since we were on a survey.

We pushed on, until we reached a huge strangler fig—a tree about 125 feet high and about 40 feet in circumference. This sounds very thick, but actually a strangler fig consists not of a single solid trunk, but of many, spread out over a considerable area. This tree, a member of the fig family, begins its life up on a branch or in the leafy crown of another tree, where seed is deposited in the excretion of birds that have eaten the fruit of other strangler figs. The seedling sends roots down to the ground along the bole of the host tree, and from some of the branches as well. The whole thing becomes an increasingly complex structure, and finally the strangler fig kills its host. The *Ficus elasticus,* as the strangler fig is called scientifically, is easily the most spectacular tree in Udjong Kulon.

Clumps of inch-thick bamboo growing every which way make a difficult barrier to pass through.

strangler fig tree, mplex structure scending roots, is d throughout the rve.

At about one o'clock Talbot and I shared a tin of tomato herring with some cold rice the men had cooked that morning for their breakfast and lunch. We finished with American cheese and raisins, washed down with cold tea. Sinaga ate with us, having a little of our menu and some of the men's.

The terrain got higher as we went on, and we came to some very pesky vegetation—huge clumps of thumb-thick bamboo,

51

which not only grew vertically but also spread out low in all directions. We had to chop a path through the tangles, and bamboo is a tough plant to cut through, even with sharp goloks. Often we cut only the bare minimum it took to allow us to get through—by crawling under the rest on hands and knees.

Late in the afternoon we crossed another stream, which may, or may not, have been the headwater of the Tjigenter. The banks were a strangely puckered limestone; the stream was fairly full and I photographed Talbot drinking from it. Away from the coast we didn't hesitate. Streams are contaminated not by nature, but by man; when humans are absent—as here, where we might have been among the first to cross or drink—there is no danger.

The forest, I'm sorry to say, was not exciting. In fact, it was almost monotonous. A botanist probably would have seen a

*Talbot drinks cl\(\)
water from a mc\(\)
tain stream edge\(\)
puckered limest\(\)*

great variety of plants, but to my amateur eye, the spectrum of plant life was very narrow—strangler figs, a vine that formed several intricate loops, and occasionally a fan-shaped species of palm (the "binbin" in Indonesian). It looks very like the kind of fan Nubians are always shown using to cool the Egyptian queen. I also saw a species of palm very much like the fishtail palm, from Florida, that I have in my New York studio.

August 13, 4 P.M.

I've just spent the last hour or so trying to photograph a small bird, feeding on the fruit of some bushes just in front of the tower. The bushes have purple blossoms, and the plant is called *Melastoma malabathricum*. Its fruit is about the size of a cherry. During my lunch, at this same table—I haven't left the tower today—I watched several birds eating this fruit. Now they're back again. They are called orange-bellied flower-peckers and are about the size of common sparrows, have orange breasts, gray bodies with black wings, and a reddish hood on their heads. They are, I'm told, the most frequent bird visitor here. Another, somewhat less frequent caller is light brown, slightly larger, and looks rather like a cedar waxwing.

Trying to photograph these birds is very frustrating. There is just enough wind to sway the outer branches and twigs of the bushes. This, coupled with the natural quick movement of the birds as they hop from one fruit to another, makes it almost impossible to focus on them with a long lens, like the 500 or 1000mm. It's just like looking for a small moving object with a telescope and then trying to make it sharp. My eyes, hands, and particularly the back of my neck are all strained from about an hour of this labor. So I've stopped and will now come back to the second day of the survey.

When I wrote about the monotony of the forest, I forgot to mention that every once in a while we did experience a total change from the unending greens—a brilliant red blossom, which the men called "hondje." This resembles the torch ginger of Hawaii closely enough to make me believe it's related. The large red flower consists of a cluster of blossoms at the end of a leafless stalk.

We didn't see any particularly interesting animals Wednesday, but Talbot did spot a small frog. He identified it as a Rhacophorus. It was 2.5 centimeters, about an inch, long, and it had beautiful golden eyes. I made several pictures of this creature, coming in very close with the 55mm Micro-Nikkor lens, which can be used as close as two inches from the subject. I tried some pictures while the frog was very lively, and then I sprayed it once with ethyl chloride to quiet it down a bit.

Talbot stopped our group at about five o'clock, and four of

the men went back to a small stream we'd crossed about an hour before, taking pails and a kettle with them to get water for our dinner. The Indonesians carry gear on a shoulder pole, like the Chinese, with equal weight in front and back. Talbot and I set up our shelter with Enang's help, had a shot of bourbon in some water from my canteen, and made our notes. Then Talbot, who's very well organized, went off a few yards and talked into his tape recorder, something he did without fail every evening. I wish I'd done the same; even after only a few days, the survey experience is a conglomerate.

Thursday, the third day of the survey, we were all up as soon as it was light. I cooked some oatmeal for Talbot and myself. While it was cooking, the sun rose over the trees around the small clearing where we were camped, and the smoke from our fire caught several narrow beams coming through the treetops. A wonderful effect—one I call cathedral lighting—was produced. Smoke or dust always makes narrow beams of light, like those from a high window in a dark interior, take specific shape. A few years ago, when I photographed a huge underground cistern on Masada, Herod's fortress on the Dead Sea, I threw fine sand and dust up into the air near the tiny window, into a beam of light. The picture was published in *Horizon,* with an account by Yigael Yadin of his digs there.

Thursday's trek started as Wednesday's had. Harum and Talbot took the lead, followed by Enang and me; the rest were about a minute behind, to lessen the noise of our passage. We all knew, though, that the steady chopping of the goloks was in itself enough to scare any animals away.

We passed a large tree the men called "bajur." Sinaga said it was *Quercus japonicus.* I know *Quercus* is oak, but this didn't look like an oak tree. Another large tree, called "kendongong" by the men, was identified by Sinaga as of the genus Spondias. I'm not too confident in these identifications. It would have been useful to have a botanist with us on the survey.

My altimeter read one hundred feet above sea level at about 11 A.M. We'd been going up and down, but obviously the terrain was ascending. I saw some small cuplike mushrooms growing out of fallen deadwood, and a little before noon, I stopped and photographed some very well-shaped ones next to our trail. But then we'd begun to cut through small stands of "tepus" (*Nicolaia sp.*), a twenty-foot-high single-stalked plant with huge leaves along both sides of its stem. This, too, looks like a member of the ginger family; Sinaga said it's one of the plants rhinoceros feed on. It spreads by putting out runners, from which it sends up a beautiful red blossom about the size of a large orchid.

Earlier Thursday, about an hour after we started, all of us

55

heard what sounded like dogs barking. But Enang whispered to me, "Kidjang." This, then, was the barking deer so called because the sound is exactly that—somewhat smaller than the deer found in the eastern U.S., about the size of an ordinary goat. We thought it would go farther away as we approached, but the sound seemed nearer and nearer as we walked on, until finally it seemed to be coming from only a few hundred feet away—too close not to halt the march and try to get a photograph.

We were in heavy underbrush, but Talbot and I reached a small clearing, leaving everyone else back on the trail. We decided that I'd wait at the edge of the clearing and give Talbot time to flank the animal, coming toward it from upwind. Hopefully, he'd alarm the deer to run downwind, toward me.

I waited, the rest of the men staying well back. I could still hear the barking for about ten minutes more while Talbot worked his way around. Then it was gone altogether.

Rice for breakfast and lunch was cooked after sunrise every day of the survey.

Soon Talbot returned, his face badly scratched by thorns—he'd made his way without cutting. To his surprise, he said, he had practically walked right into not one, but two deer. The animals looked him over quite calmly. Then, before they ran off—and nowhere near the clearing—the male snarled at him, pulling up his upper lip to reveal his teeth, an action that's typical of this animal. I should have gone with Talbot, but no one can predict these events in advance. All very frustrating.

About midday we came to a large strangler fig on a small elevation, and Harum climbed up its aerial structure. We hoped he'd get a glimpse of the sea so that we could check our position. But we were too far inland—well into the interior of the sanctuary—for him to spot it.

We reached an altitude of about two hundred feet by mid-afternoon, and found a different species of bamboo; the stem has a diameter of about four inches. I think the bamboo is one of the most beautiful of all plants, and so do the Japanese. It is one of their favorite subjects for ink drawings and through it they are able to convey serenity.

We made our third camp, and Talbot and I had our by now usual drink, then a makeshift meal—this time, a can of pork and beans fortified with canned frankfurters and served over the rice everyone was having. Talbot and I talked for a long time that evening, each under his own mosquito net. Between us, where either could reach, were a flask of bourbon, a canteen of water, a bug bomb, a flashlight, and the Walther pistol. Over our heads stretched the tarpaulin, cutting out the sky.

We talked about Africa that evening. Talbot knows it well, is even an honorary white hunter in Kenya. We've both been to many places in Africa. The same places often—but at different times. I supposed that explained why we hadn't met before. Still, as one story led to another, until we finally fell asleep, it seemed strange that we hadn't crossed trails earlier.

Friday, the fourth day, was the most interesting of all. First there was the problem of where we were. Talbot believed it was time to change our course and go northwest toward Tjidaon tower; Sinaga didn't agree with him. We had no landmarks, but Talbot was basing his judgment on how many hours we had walked and also on the few elevations marked on the map. Harum climbed another strangler fig, but again couldn't spot the sea. Talbot decided to make the turn northward. That was around noon.

Earlier, before we turned, a mouse deer—these deer are only about a foot high—reacted to our noise by practically flying across our path. I didn't even see what it was—just a blur. I'd already realized that there was no chance to get any animal pictures while we were chopping our way through the jungle.

But I was nevertheless very disappointed.

Friday seemed to be the animal day. Harum was in the lead, chopping away when Talbot spotted—in a place Harum had already passed—some bones almost covered by dead leaves. We stopped and began to search, and soon cries of "Badak! Badak!" were coming from all sides. We'd found part of the skeleton of an adult rhinoceros. Soon we had the entire skull. This was measured, then carefully packed. Dry leaves were used as padding.

We collected as many bones as we could find and piled them together in the event that they were to be picked up later by Game Department personnel. Talbot and Sinaga kept a careful eye on the men, since rhinoceros bones of any kind are valuable in Indonesia. The Chinese believe that powdered rhino horn, actually stiff hairs hardened together, is the greatest male aphrodisiac going. Many rhinos are killed illegally in Kenya and Tanzania for this.

Indonesians will buy *any* part of a rhino—meat, skin, bones, anything. They think the whole animal is magical. We therefore had to forbid the men to collect any bones for themselves.

Talbot measures the skull of an adult rhinoceros that may have been killed by poachers.

...ot and Sinaga ...gree about our ...tion on the fourth ...while Harum ...bs for a bearing.

When we found the bones we were at an elevation of about 300 feet. An hour or so later, at four o'clock, we were still climbing. My altimeter read 375 feet. Suddenly Harum froze in his tracks and pointed to a treetop up ahead. I stared and stared, then used my five-power binoculars, to no avail.

Finally Talbot, who'd seen it immediately, pointed out a flying lemur hugging a branch. He was enormously excited. No one had ever photographed this species before, and I had my camera ready.

I waited for the creature to take flight—the flying lemur has a wide area of skin between its legs and can glide through the air from one tree to another. This one didn't move for about ten minutes. So after a few shots of it in the tree, where it blended all too well into the background, I had the men begin to throw pieces of wood at it. I wasn't using a motor drive on my Nikon; a motor drive lets you keep shooting automatically, as you would with a movie camera, but it's much too noisy for the jungle, and also, it takes too many pictures too quickly. Still, I wish I'd had it then, because when the flying lemur finally took off, I'd just finished a shot of it at rest and wasn't quite ready for its sail. I did get one shot of it before it reached the next tree, but I don't know how well the photo, made with a 200mm lens, and by pure reflex action on my part, will come out.

We continued our march, and at 4:45 stumbled into a well-cut trail heading almost due north. It was one of Dr. Schenkel's, Talbot said; searching for rhinoceros, Schenkel and his men had cut many. Finding it made everything simple. We knew the tower was only a few hours away, and we made camp near the trail. I slept easy that night, knowing the survey was just about over.

A long-tailed agamid lizard waits for insects, which it catches with its tongue.

*g lemur has
ane between its
nd back legs
ables it to glide.*

In spite of my hurry to reach the tower, I was pleased by an interruption that took place the next morning when I found a small green lizard. This was a very photogenic creature, with bright green scales, a very long tail, and nasty looking teeth. Since the lizard kept its mouth open all the time, the teeth were constantly displayed. I made a long shot showing the lizard's entire length, then an extreme close-up of its head. As it obligingly held still, I kept taking shot after shot. This was near the beach, for our trail didn't lead us to the tower itself, but east of it, out on the shore.

When we finally reached the sea, Sohib, our cook, was so thrilled that he ran into it fully clothed. I was tempted to follow him in, but waited for a hot shower at the tower. As I noted earlier, my first act on getting to the tower was to open the refrigerator. Talbot and I had a beer, then Talbot spent the rest of the day listening to the other group leaders report their find-

Larger-than-life-s close-up makes harmless agamid lizard look danger

Sohib runs happily into the sea after five hot days of cutting through the forest.

ings. (The other groups, having had shorter distances to cover, were back before us.) The written reports were collected and will be assessed later by Talbot.

I listened to some of the men's reports, then stopped to assess my own results. I had exposed sixteen rolls of film, fourteen high-speed Ektachrome and two Kodachrome. I knew that I'd have to ask Talbot to carry a cable to Djakarta when he leaves —he's going Friday—asking *Life* to ship in more Ektachrome. I don't have too much to show for the five days of the survey. At least I don't think I do. A good photographer knows when he clicks the shutter what the results will be. I have some nice things, but nothing spectacular. I don't have two great pictures to use to open and close the story—and these are essential for an important essay. But I'm not worried. I have several months to go.

I've decided—in fact, I'd already half decided this when I first set out for Java—that I'm not going to track or chase animals, but let them come to me. Robert Ardrey explained in *The Territorial Imperative* how male animals choose a territory and defend it against other males. Ardrey and I worked together in East Africa for an ABC Africa show. Since I believe in his idea, I'm planning on finding the territory of each animal species I want, building a blind there, and staying in the blind—even living in it—until the animals come to me.

Wednesday, August 16, 1:30 P.M.

Talbot, Harum, Enang, and I are back at the tower after a two-day sortie to the Tjibunar, a large river that empties from the south coast into the sea. Dr. Schenkel and his men had already cut a trail across the sanctuary to this point, and we were able to walk without cutting.

Talbot, Sinaga, and the author are joined by six trackers and porters for the Tjibunar sortie.

Talbot has just diluted his bourbon with jibunar water after a long hot walk.

It was only a three-hour walk, but would have taken two days if the trail hadn't been cut. There is one steep hill to be climbed, both up and down. Down is more difficult, though less strenuous—gravity helps you fall.

The first animal we surprised on the trail was a banteng cow. I got just one shot, then she bounded out of sight. Since there was no cutting to be done, and the trail was clearly indicated, I could be, and was, lead man. Often I couldn't see what was making the dead leaves move, and it worried me. I'm not afraid of snakes, but it's comforting to have someone else go first and tell them to leave. They almost always do.

A little reptile, a brown skink with a yellow band on its side, liked the lower vegetation of the trail. I scared one after the other into scurrying away; then I finally caught one, which I photographed on a log. This creature is of the genus Eumeces, Talbot informed me.

The only other animal I photographed was a good-sized wild

A wild pig is surprised eating shellfish at the mouth of the Tjibunar

pig. He was browsing in the sweet water of the Tjibunar, just near its exit to the sea, and I made several pictures of him before he caught our scent. These pigs eat all sorts of shellfish, including a very good-sized clam resembling the Atlantic quahog; the sand was littered with empty shells.

Some univalves we found adhering to the rocks at low tide were rather like small abalones. Yesterday we collected some, steamed them, and ate them for lunch.

The Tjibunar is a pretty river for the quarter of a mile before it goes into the ocean. It meanders around several low meadows of bright green grass and sparkles over clean rocks and pebbles. After Talbot and I found a suitable deep depression in the river-bed to bathe in, we wasted no time in removing our clothes. Talbot kept his safari hat on though. Why, I don't know, since he does have a good head of hair to protect his scalp from the sun.

I put a good shot of bourbon in each of our cups and we added some of the river water to it as we soaked ourselves in the cool stream.

The remnants of what had once been a game-observation tower stood alongside the Tjibunar. But the tower was in such bad shape that we didn't dare sleep in or under it. Instead we pitched a tarpaulin about fifteen feet from the beach, where a stand of pandanus trees sheltered us against the wind.

At dawn today I started down to the beach to spend a penny, then stopped short. Just outside our camp there were fresh leopard tracks. The tracks went right past the camp, however, without interruption or change of direction—an indication of the animal's lack of interest in us. Leopards prey on pigs, monkeys, and peacocks.

We followed the shore eastward, going through large stands of pandanus, the tree Polynesians call "lahala" (it's also called screw pine) and use to make their mats and huts. The pandanus has an aerial root system shaped like a triangle. This helps support it on coral and sandy soil. The fruit, which is pineapplelike in appearance—but not taste—is eaten by Micronesians, who have very little to choose from; it is not eaten by Indonesians.

Wednesday, August 16, 3:30 P.M.

I've just returned from photographing Suleman removing thorns from his legs with the tip of a machete. I also made some close-ups of his legs, showing the tick infections most of the men have. Kiflie has so many on his buttocks that he's having trouble walking straight.

Tomorrow night we're going over to Peutjang to have dinner with the Schenkels, since Talbot is leaving the day after tomorrow. They sent a note inviting us and saying they would send

Fresh leopard tracks less than a hundred feet from our Tjibunar camp were not reassuring.

pandanus trees a low group of roots to help rt them on thin

their launch, the *Badak*, for him at five and expected me at six. I know they want to talk to him about their work, since he is connected with the World Wildlife Fund, the organization sponsoring their stay, but I feel rather cut by their sending the *Badak* for him and not for me. I'm to go over on the *Harini*.

Thursday, August 17

Today Talbot and I inspected the blind Amir and Kiflie have built for me a hundred or so yards in front of the tower. The blind is almost in the middle of a grazing field that's about five acres in size. The field is being cleared of all its small bushes and shrubs to give the grass a chance to grow and make it more attractive to bantengs, peacocks, monkeys, pigs, and other herbivorous animals. Dr. Schenkel is supervising a group of about twenty Indonesians who're doing the clearing.

The field directly in front of the tower was cut about a month ago. This gave us good visibility, as well as animals to work with, right from the day we arrived.

The blind is a small hut with head-high walls built from

Suleman digs thorns from his feet and shows the scars from infected tick bites on his legs.

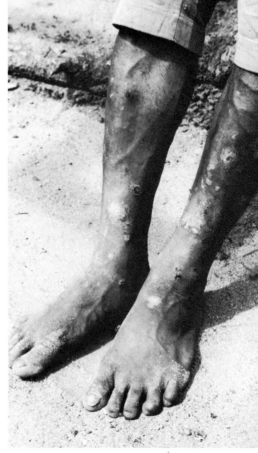

local trees and bushes—live bushes, some of them. Holes have been cut into the walls so I can aim and shoot a camera without being seen. When Talbot and I had completed our inspection and were satisfied, he made some Polaroid pictures of me in the blind to take back to New York.

Friday, August 18, 10 A.M.

Talbot left earlier this morning on the *Badak,* which is making its fortnightly run to Labuan. He took with him the exposed film, which had been kept in the refrigerator, and the mail and cables for New York. It wasn't easy to see him go. Now I'm alone with the Indonesians—all wonderful people, but different in many ways from me. Sinaga can speak adequate English, but he's not eager to strain himself socially in a foreign language.

I don't know how long I'll have to stay in Udjong Kulon. But I'm willing to face up to it. Before Talbot left, he and I had worked out a list of possible targets for the story and planned a group of sorties that should give me maximum coverage of the sanctuary. I'm starting on the first of these sorties in just an hour or so.

Yesterday evening was very pleasant. The Schenkels live in a frame house made from hand-sawn lumber. The interior walls are woven bamboo, the furnishings adequate.

Usually the local game warden's wife cooks for the Schenkels but yesterday a young scientist from the Game Department, Widodo, and Djuhari, the chief game warden of the sanctuary, who lives and has his headquarters in Labuan, prepared the meal. They were excellent cooks; the meal was easily the best I've ever had so far in Indonesia. There were two fish dishes; then there was chicken in a sort of curry sauce, served with different vegetables; finally there was a wonderful fruit salad of bananas, papaya, mangoes, and oranges the Schenkels had brought from Bogor, where they spend a week every month doing their research. I brought them a bottle of Chablis, which was very welcome.

Both the Schenkels are enthusiasts, even to loving one of their chickens, a rooster they call Hansie, whom they can't bear to kill; last night he came into their house to say hello.

The Schenkels' presence on Peutjang is very reassuring on several counts. They can help if something happens—help with their knowledge, and also, help with their boat, the *Badak.* They know more—much more than I do—about the flora and fauna of Udjong Kulon and can advise me. And they're good company. The only problem is they are almost constantly on the move, going out for several days at a time to study rhinoceros, and also leaving the sanctuary entirely for a week every month.

71

I've arranged for the Schenkels to carry the next bunch of film to Djakarta when they go to Bogor two weeks from now. Talbot is to inform Amir Daud, the *Time-Life* part-time correspondent there, not to send a car to Labuan on September 1, as I'd asked him to do before Talbot and I left for Udjong Kulon. Because there's no communication with the outside from the sanctuary, plans like these have to be formulated carefully. Talbot will explain to Daud and set up another relay, for September 15, so that my next batch of film, which will be Take 3—each batch is numbered—will be picked up.

Talbot plans to spend several days in Djakarta on scientific business, and before he left this morning, we decided I'd send the *Harini* to Labuan in a few days. Since the *Badak* is coming right back to the sanctuary, there won't be time to put aboard my mail, which is waiting in Djakarta, or the supplies Talbot volunteered to get for me there. Also, I want the answers to the

Dr. Schenkel's twin-engine launch, the Badak, *tows a disabled sailing canoe offshore.*

cables Talbot's sending to New York for me, and several days will be needed for the exchange to take place.

En route to Labuan the *Harini* will drop some of the men in Tamandjaja; they'll be picked up on the way back here. These men are married and have small farms, so their occasional presence at home is necessary. I intend to let some men go and come back with each trip the *Harini* makes.

Sunday, August 20, 5 P.M.

I am back in the Tjidaon tower after a two-and-a-half-day

sortie to the western tip of the sanctuary. We went along the coast—on the sand when the tide was out, and on a path through the low bushes paralleling the edge of the sea when the tide was in. Within two hours we reached the mouth of the Tjiramea. We passed a smaller stream en route; its water was too salty to drink or to cook in.

We camped not too far from the lighthouse that flashes a beacon to ships going through the Sunda Strait, which is between Sumatra and Java and provides a passageway from Ceylon to Singapore. Beside the lighthouse there's a deep well with adequate water. About a half mile away, in a more sheltered bay, is a landing pier built of stone by the Dutch so they could supply men working in the area. The Dutch also constructed a road, of coral, from the pier to the lighthouse and lined both sides with yellow-flowering trees. The trees were

The lighthouse on the extreme western tip of Udjong Kulon marks one side of the Sunda Strait.

planted long ago, and those that are left are of good size. Unfortunately, no one cares for them now; Indonesia's independence was proclaimed in 1945 (after the departure of the Japanese, who occupied it from 1942 to 1945), and since then—or possibly somewhat before then—at least half of the trees have either been knocked down by storms or killed by strangler figs. Before inspecting the lighthouse itself, I made some photographs of yellow-tailed squirrels in and near the trees.

The lighthouse is a steel tower about seventy-five feet tall. It stands on the highest promontory on the western end of the island. Around it is a group of tin-roofed stone buildings; huge steel cisterns filled by rain falling on the roofs are connected to each other by pipes.

This view of the western shore was taken from halfway up the lighthouse tower.

I tried to climb the tower, even after noticing that the iron rungs and uprights of its ladder were very rusted. After reaching the second stage—the tower is in three parts—I decided I'd had enough. The iron was almost all gone and I'd have felt rather foolish trusting my weight to what was left. Since I didn't need high elevation pictures of the Sunda Strait, I made a few shots from where I was and let it go at that.

Overleaf:
Cormorants and terns nest on the guano-covered islands off the western shore.

The sortie had two main targets. The first was simple: a group of very exciting small, high islands—the Schenkels told me of them—that are covered with bird colonies. The Schenkels also mentioned big waves breaking against the island rocks, with spectacular effects. The second target was a rhino wallow about a half hour's climb up the hill that forms the crest of Java's western end. A wallow is a depression in the land that fills up with enough water during a heavy rain to produce a large mud bath. Since rhinos love to lie in the mud, and since they also come to this particular wallow to drink from the clearer portion, for there are no rivers on the hill, this is a perfect place to wait for them.

Three trails had been made by the rhinos to the wallow. The depth of the trails told of their frequent use.

I decided to send a work party back to the wallow to build a blind, and Sinaga and I selected three trees to use for a small tree house. The trees overlook the north side of the wallow, so the wind will be from it to the blind; also, the trees are on a small height, so the blind will have an elevation of about twenty feet, enough for my cameras to clear any shrubs in the foreground.

I devoted the rest of my time at the western end to photographing the bird islands. It is difficult to try to describe the beauty and power of the surf in relation to the abruptly high islands, which are shaped like giant wedding cakes topped with what looks like white icing. The birds, most of which are cormorants, and as black as those in Maine when seen against the sun, look artificial and arranged along the islands' tops. I'd have liked to get close to the islands, but no boat could have survived the surrounding surf, so I worked from the shore.

I went to sleep early Saturday evening and woke early in the morning, when I was very happy to learn that during the night Enang and Harum had captured a huge sea turtle. She was laying, or about to lay, her eggs on the beach when they found her. To prevent her from going back into the sea, they simply turned her over on her back. When I got down to the beach, there she was waving her flippers and going nowhere.

It was quite a job for Enang and Harum to turn her back over again; she weighed, I'd guess, several hundred pounds. When they'd accomplished it, she started down the beach, back

to the sea, and I got lots of pictures of her "flight."

The turtle would have made many wonderful meals for us, but we were strictly forbidden to hunt, kill, or eat any of the local animals. I didn't find any turtle eggs, though I examined several tracks—they resembled those of a Patton tank—along the beach. Perhaps the turtle couldn't made up her mind to lay or not. Perhaps the men had interrupted her by turning her over. In any case, she seemed very glad to go back into the sea.

On our way back to the tower after lunch, a high tide forced us to the forest, where, not far from the Tjiramea, we found an old rhino print. I also saw, and also photographed, a sort of basket fern that grows on the branches of a tree that's called "njamplung" in Indonesian; my checklist identified the tree as *Calophyllum inophyllum,* a very heavy balsam with a wide crown and stiff leathery leaves. This tree is most common near the shore. Not far from the tree in which I found the fern was another, smaller tree, a wild hibiscus. Wild hibiscus, which are called "hau" in Polynesia, are found all over the Pacific. They have yellow flowers, and their bark, removed in narrow strips, is often used like cord.

Huge sea turtles lay hundreds of soft eggs in the sand and then return to the sea.

The trip back was uneventful after finding the rhino print. We reached the tower at 3:30 this afternoon, well before dark.

Monday, August 21, 5 P.M.

I am on the *Harini,* and finding it a little difficult to write. I've just tried—unsuccessfully—to photograph the fruit bat colony that lives on the northern end of Peutjang island. There are some high rocks at this point, and because one has a huge hole in it, the point is called Kerangtjopong which means the rock with the hole. The failure was my fault—bad planning.

Harum and I were landed on the shore in a small dugout canoe at the start of the operation. There was a strong surf, and the canoe was handled by a man from the lighthouse who had come to see me about getting his ten-year-old son to Labuan on the *Harini's* next trip. He was a small-boat expert if I ever saw one, watching each wave and choosing just the right one to make his landing—not on a beach, but in a narrow cut in a large bed of coral bordering the island. Very tricky with cameras to carry. One of my waterproof sacks was punctured on the sharp coral during this landing.

Harum and I reached the trees where the bats were peacefully hanging upside down, their normal position, and they rose into the air at our screams, but the foliage blocked my view, and the pictures, I knew right then and there, will be unsatisfactory.

To make things worse, when we reached the *Harini,* we were told that thousands of flying foxes, as fruit bats are sometimes called, had sailed right over the crews' heads.

Next time I'll wait on the *Harini,* send a man to shore with a walkie-talkie—and be ready when he spooks the bats off their branches. They are normally nocturnal and go off to feed at dusk. Not much use to me.

A little too difficult to write with this boat rocking around so.

Tuesday, August 22

I am on the mainland again and camping—for the afternoon— in the blind a hundred or so yards from the tower. It's just 3 P.M. and I've been here since 2:30 adjusting the leaves around the north aperture. Because the leaves left on the cut branches from which the blind was built dried out quickly, leaving large gaps in the wall, I've had Harum and Enang line the inside of the blind with a palm curtain—the same kind of solid curtain I'm using in the tower to stop the wind from blasting through.

It blows hard most of the time—gusts up to 20 or 30 knots. But I'm not complaining, for it is this wind which cools down the heat enough so that I can sleep—on top of, not in, my sleeping bag. I put the air mattress inside the sleeping bag, cover myself with a single sheet, and am fairly comfortable. But I do

have a problem in sleeping though—caused by a type of bed-bug which behaves like a close relative. I've had a bed built of bamboo, well off the floor and in contact with no walls. Each leg of the bed is sitting in a tin can filled with kerosene, so the bugs can't come up from the floor. Above and around me each night is a mosquito net suspended from four posts, so the bugs which can't get at me from below, can't do it from above either. Yet they do get to me. How. . . ?

I checked the entire setup today, then moved the bed two inches away from the bamboo table, then sprayed everything, including my sleeping bag. I hope tomorrow morning I won't have any new bites. The fact that I killed a small scorpion on the floor last night is not reassuring.

A minute ago, when I put a few extra leaves around the 1000mm lens, which is just barely sticking out of the blind in the direction from which a group of five bantengs—four females, one of them with a baby—likes to emerge from the forest, I thought back to a story I did on Maria Callas. I put a Nikon with a long lens and a radio-operated motor in a bank of ferns in front of the orchestra at Maxim's after her opening at the Opéra in Paris. I pasted some leaves on the tripod and the body of the camera and sat at a nearby table in black tie. Every time she and Onassis leaned toward each other I pushed a button on a little box in my lap. This activated a receiver on the camera and clicked the mechanism. I did this only during loud music, which is infrequent at Maxim's.

The bantengs were here yesterday before I left for Peutjang, but only the mother ventured out of the bush at the edge of the forest. They didn't see me, and since the wind was strongly from them, I don't think they could have smelled me either. It is so dry the grass in the open is very scarce, and they were grazing on low bushes. I spent this morning writing picture captions and photographing from the tower window, but the bantengs were too far away to get. Here in the blind, which is halfway across the clearing, should be better.

Wednesday, August 23

I'm in the blind again. Yesterday I was here from 2:30 to 5:30, and finally got a couple of fine close-ups of a peahen. She was so close to the blind that I was amazed she didn't mind several clicks before she went about her feeding.

This morning I succeeded in attracting a small dragon—a monitor lizard at least five feet long, who couldn't resist the smell of a dead chicken I hung near the tower. He came very slowly and with many pauses, and I was tracking him all the time, first with the 1000mm lens, then the 500mm, and finally the 300. All from above him in the tower. His tongue forked out

Fruit bats, sometimes called flying foxes, hang upside down on the high trees of Peutjang Island.

81

so quickly, and went back so fast, that I'm not quite sure I have any shots of him with it out. At the beginning I have a very mysterious group showing him hiding behind a bush; you can see his eye between the twigs. In one shot of this group part of his body and tail are visible.

Before the lizard appeared, a pair of chestnut-headed bee-eaters (*Merops viridis*) played near me. It is now 3:30, and they haven't returned—or if they have, I haven't been able to spot them from the blind. It doesn't matter; at the moment I'm after bigger game.

Things are quite different with Talbot gone. We used to talk after dinner; now I'm alone. I try using my Sony three-band radio to get *The Voice of America*. I had Ella Fitzgerald last night, but lousy reception; and I couldn't get Mulligan in a Moscow jam session with a borrowed sax—too much static. Sammy Davis, Jr., is supposed to be on twice this week, live from Vegas, but I doubt if I'll be able to hear him; the best I can do usually is understand what they're saying on the news.

Some of the men from Tamandjaja are home now. The *Harini*, which I sent to Labuan Monday evening (after I got back from Peutjang) to pick up my mail, cables, and the supplies I asked

A monitor lizard over five feet long is attracted by fish bones left near the tower as bait.

Talbot to buy when he was in Djakarta, was to drop the men in Tamandjaja, which is along the way. They're to bring back eggs, twelve chickens, and fresh vegetables—potatoes, cabbage, onions, carrots, tomatoes, and cucumbers. We'll have to eat most of the vegetables quickly, but I'll try to save some in the refrigerator, although it is almost filled with film.

Bless that kerosene refrigerator! It has made some difference. I use half cans of food and save the rest, keep extra fish and leftover chicken, chill the boiled water, and even have some beautiful Chablis. But I'm hardly dining in luxury, as witness my lunch today: some tasteless Danish frankfurters cut up into a can of pork and beans. I doctored this mixture with garlic and onion powder, Worcestershire sauce, mustard, brown sugar, cider vinegar, and a few splashes of a hot sauce I made by steeping chili peppers in gin (in a tiny miniature Drambuie bottle, courtesy Air India).

Last night I cooked the rice—Sohib, the regular cook, is one of the men who're in Tamandjaja. Sinaga and Amir were amazed that I used a whole pot of water for a small amount of rice; they cover the rice to a certain height and then boil the water away, leaving a glutinous mass. They even admitted to liking rice this new way.

When I first came to the tower, the field in front was much more active. There were peacocks in full plumage, monkeys, and the banteng group. Now the fact that the tower is occupied seems to have made the animals somewhat wary; also, there is almost no grass left for them to feed on. I keep trying, and think, sooner or later, I'm bound to get something good—like the crack I had at the lizard this morning.

4 P.M. I just looked, and a troop of gray monkeys appeared. They're a little far away, even for the 1000mm, but I made some shots of them anyway, in a tree where they seem to be eating bright yellow petals; one of the monkeys is also holding a green fruit. The tree—called a "sempur" by the men—has a few large leaves, some fruit, and a very few bright yellow flowers; in size and shape it looks rather like the West Indian flamboyant. The monkeys are macaques. They're a good size, but nowhere near that of chimps.

4:20. No bantengs yet, but I've just spent ten minutes with a very vain peahen, not the same one I saw yesterday. This one sat down about a hundred yards from me and preened herself, poking her head under her tail, her wings—wherever it could reach. This for about three to four seconds; then up comes the head, sharply, and looks around for possible danger; then down goes the head again. Quite a wonderful head, and nice glint on the body as well. Wish she'd come closer for a full-frame shot.

She may.

83

I waited on the deck of the *Harini* from 8:30 to 10:30—and the crew couldn't start the engine, even with the hand crank. I then discovered that the regular mechanic had been left behind in Labuan and the owner's young nephew is replacing him. Tjibun, the owner's agent, says the nephew is a fine mechanic and that the older man wanted some extra days in Labuan. We'll see, for Ong claims the nephew can fix the engine in about five hours.

I suspect the owner simply wants his relative along.

If they can't start the engine, I'm really in trouble, since the only way to cover the peninsula is to go on the boat to a point on the shore where you wish to penetrate and then go in. There are so many hills and ravines that if I tried to work from the tower, it would take days to move a few miles. I am not very happy right now.

Friday, August 25, 8 A.M.

On board the *Harini*. The engine now starts. At least, it's fixed for the moment.

I checked and found out that although the boat is fairly new, the engine is from a 1952 Dodge truck. The *Harini* is twelve meters long, four meters wide, and can carry ten tons. So says Ong Tjinbun.

Ong is small and wears a jacket and trousers of jungle cloth and a khaki beret—for which he'll substitute any borrowed hat he can get. The lighthouseman had a sailor hat, so Ong wore that while the man was aboard. The day the survey teams were getting ready, Ong carried one of the rifles. This morning he carried a guitar (without playing it) that belongs to one of the men cutting trails for Dr. Schenkel. He's quite a character. He and his crew are paid about $25 a day, whether the *Harini* runs or not. The cheapest yacht I ever hired.

The last time I tried to charter a yacht in the Pacific I was in Tahiti doing photos of the "literary" South Seas for *Life*. I needed to do the Tuamotus (also called the Low Islands and the Dangerous Archipelago), which were made famous by Nordhoff and Hall's *The Hurricane*, then to continue from there to the Marquesas, where Herman Melville jumped a whaler and was captured by the cannibal Typee people on the island of Nuku Hiva. Melville wrote a great book, *Typee*, about this. On another Marquesan island, Hiva Oa, Gauguin died and was buried.

8:55 A.M. Great excitement aboard—we ran into a mob of sharp-tailed terns, seemingly smaller than those in Maine, which were diving into the water after a school of small fish. Had to guess focus with the 200mm, used Kodachrome for maximum brilliance of birds against water, shoreline, and sky.

wearing a jungle-uniform, proudly ~ys a "tongkol" ~t by the Harini

Some large fish were also chasing the same school, and one of the *Harini's* crew ran out a line and trolled behind the boat. He used a strip of the white stem of a spider lily (called "bakung" here) as a plug. Part of it is cut into shreds and then rolled up; the hook is inserted in the solid end; the slit pieces become a waving tail.

He just caught one of the big fish. The men call it a "tongkol"; to me it looks like an albacore or bonito. My guess is that it weighs about eight or nine pounds. They say this is the best eating fish in these waters. I'll know more about that tonight.

9:05. Reached Kerantjopong, but no fruit bats visible. We are cruising back and forth looking.

August 25, 3:30 P.M.

I'm back at the tower now, writing again. I'm becoming more and more interested in this diary. I know it will mean something to my daughters, Elin and Jill, and possibly be interesting to others too. Perhaps only the fact that I have no one to talk to prompts this effort. If so, so be it.

I spent yesterday afternoon in the blind but I didn't record what happened. I'm sorry now, for trying to write about it today isn't the same as writing about it while it's going on.

I'm not sure about what I photographed yesterday. I did see

A pied hornbill also eats the yellow petals of the "sempur" tree near the author's blind.

a lot. The big problem was that Amir stupidly came out to the blind, in a white shirt yet, with a message from the Schenkels. This stopped all animal activity for more than an hour. Luckily it resumed, but late in the afternoon when the light was rather low. For the first time, the banteng group of five, including the baby, came right out into the open. I was exposing at 1/30 second with the fixed aperture F11-1000mm mirror lens. Even with the camera on a firm tripod, this slow shutter speed may have vibrated the camera too much for a 20X magnification. I hope several—at least—of the shots are sharp, because there was one moment when two large females stood side by side and looked toward me—with the baby well in the clear.

I also did a family of wild pigs yesterday. The males have wonderful manes—stiff hair along the back of the neck. I got several good shots, with the 1000mm, including a profile of the biggest pig with his mouth wide open as he munched at something in the field. It was quite an afternoon. Two peafowl—hens possibly, but certainly not full-grown cocks—walked together and posed for a few shots; also, a small hornbill flapped into the yellow-blossoming tree and enjoyed some of its petals.

On my way back to the tower I tasted one of the petals. I thought it would be very sweet, since monkeys, peacocks, and now hornbills eat the yellow flowers. But I found it bitter.

The Schenkels came by at 5:45, just as I came back from the blind, and I thanked them again for having had the field cut. Charles Lindbergh, when he was here this year, donated the money to have this done.

Now that I've caught up with yesterday, I'd better go back to the yacht in the South Seas—before it gets lost in the shuffle. I'm not sure these digressions won't ruin my account of Udjong Kulon, but it seems to want to write itself this way.

I had heard that the Seventh Day Adventists had a large schooner in Papeete which they used for proselytizing the people of the outer islands. I went to see the head of the mission, a two-year-term volunteer who was quite ready to rent the boat for something like $400 a week—if he could go along to spread the Word. I agreed. Then he said, "The boat is like our temple—no smoking and no alcohol." The whisky injunction was a real blow but I agreed. And then he said, "of course no coffee or tea." This was too much, especially when I checked the waterfront and found that the schooner's skipper had blown out his sails on the last trip.

I finally took passage on a filthy but wonderful copra schooner (copra—dried coconut meat—is exported and made into coconut oil) and had a plane fly out from Papeete to meet the schooner and take me back from the Marquesas. This took some doing. It was worth it. I went into the Typee valley, found the sacred hula ground and the huge stone tikis, described by Melville, climbed Temiteu, the mountain Gauguin included in most of his Marquesan compositions (one is in the Boston Museum), and saw Gauguin's grave.

Getting back this morning, the trip to Peutjang island was not a great success. The best of it was sighting the terns diving for fish. Crossing the island I saw at least thirty wild pigs, about twenty rusa deer, several small gray monkeys, and one peahen. No fruit bats.

I did some photography, but the deer were always hidden in brush thick enough to ruin any good picture possibilities. It was also so dark, even at midday, and almost at the equator, that I was trying to use the 200mm lens at 1/60 second. This with the camera hand held, as any noise or glitter from a tripod would have scattered the deer away. I was within a hundred feet of several, but don't believe I have anything worthwhile. If I am to get rusa deer, I'll have to build a blind and wait them out. One stupid pig which was half asleep in a cozy little pit of fine sand he had dug for his siesta let me walk practically right up to him before the wind veered and he caught my scent.

I am sitting now at the tower window facing the east, watching our cleared field for animals. So far, only peahens—and I'm fed up with them. I need a prancing male.

Four men erected this blind in several hours using branches fastened with stripped rattan runners and covered it with woven arenga palm fronds.

Just met with Sinaga and arranged for us to move out on a three-day sortie to the Tjigenter. We'll take the *Harini*—or rather, she will take us, Sinaga, myself, and six men—to the shore near the river mouth opposite Handeuleum island. A game warden lives on Handeuleum, but the Schenkels tell me the warden's house is infested with rats and bedbugs, so I'm taking my L. L. Bean tent.

I usually camp about fifty feet from the men—they seem to prefer it, and I find it quieter. It is a little hairy when you know there are leopards about. I originally intended to bring a buck-shot-loaded twelve-gauge pump gun to Java, the same gun I took to Africa during the gorilla expedition, but Talbot said licenses and so forth would be too complicated. I do have the Walther .765 automatic, and I've been placing it near my head at night, next to my flashlight, roll of toilet paper, and bug bomb. But the Walther in the jungle doesn't amount to much more than a lion tamer's cap pistol at the circus. Also, guns can be dangerous to others. I'll never forget the night, earlier this year, our ABC camera crew was camping on a broken-down farm in the Congo. George Wittman, an ex-lieutenant colonel in the Army Special Services and our superb consultant on the Congo, was along for that part of the trip, which was through

The author sits in the finished blind, his cameras close at hand, but nothing comes.

Mulele rebel country between Bukavu and Kindu. At Kindu Italian aviators had recently been killed and eaten by the rebels. I shared a room with George, went out quite noiselessly to spend a penny, and then I came back in. As I entered the room, George sat up suddenly and pointed a .38 revolver right at me. I hit the deck before identifying myself. I remembered that Colonel Marcus, an American who went to Israel to train its army in guerrilla warfare, had been killed by one of his own men in just such circumstances.

I never carry the Walther out; in fact, none of the men knows I have it. It's in an old khaki oblong pouch on my belt, and since I carry Mercurochrome and Band-Aids in the same case, everyone thinks it's my first-aid kit. It could be.

August 25, 5:20 P.M.

I've just been out trying to catch up to a beautiful peacock— the very one I need. But he kept going into deep shadow before I could get him. Anyway, I need the sun glistening on that wonderful neck and head.

This particular peacock seems to have a specific territory to the right of the tower and between it and the blind. So before I came in now, I ordered a small blind, just for him, in the middle of his territory. Anyone who has read Robert Ardrey's *Territorial Imperative* knows how important territory is to the animal world. A male picks out an area and will fight another who invades it. Females are always welcome, however. In Africa last year, on the Serengeti plains, I saw the small Thomson's gazelles marking the edges of their territories by rubbing twig tops against a special gland beneath their eyes. The gland, which looks like a black stripe, secretes a thick black scented fluid, which sticks to the twigs. Each gazelle has his own scent, and once he has deposited it, he has marked his ground.

Saturday, August 26, 10 A.M.

We boarded the *Harini* at 9:15 this morning and were under way at 9:30.

We were supposed to leave at 8 A.M., but I noticed last night that the "sempur" tree's yellow flowers, which the hornbills, monkeys, and peacocks had been eating, were almost finished, and I wanted to take some more photographs before the flowers were completely gone.

The tree is a peculiar one. Most of its leaves have fallen; the few that are left are about 40 centimeters long, oblate in shape, and coarsely textured. The blossoms are 15.5 centimeters across from petal tip to petal tip, a brilliant cadmium yellow. Each flower has five petals, about the shape and size of those of the flamboyant, arranged around a ring of what I think are stamens

94

or rudimentary ones and an innermost core, flat and round, that seems to be the pistil. The fruit, which looks something like a green fig, is almost full grown on flowerless parts of the tree. So the tree has some old leaves, some flowers, and some fruit, all at once. Another strange tree here has clusters of small plum-sized fruits all over its trunk, even close to the ground. The curved branches of the "sempur" [which was identified later as *Dillenia aurea*] make photographing it very exciting; without really trying, I got compositions resembling those of Japanese flower paintings, especially those of the Momoyama period.

Every time I come on board the *Harini,* the crew is cooking or has just finished cooking, fish, which the men eat with boiled rice. This three times a day. Almost always fish and rice, which they try to make different ways. Yesterday it was served with a yellowish sauce, not very hot and quite good.

As soon as I came on today, there was a very good smell from the galley. "Galley" is rather a grand word for it. The

Fish is cooked twice a day in a special box on the deck of the Harini.

95

cooking area is, as it is on most small vessels (even canoes in Africa), on deck, with something to keep the fire in its own spot. On the *Harini* this something is a large wooden crate, open at the top and front, with diamond-shaped openings in the two sides. The crate stands on a brick platform a foot or so high, and most of its bottom has been cut away, providing a brick surface on which to build the fire. Four brick posts are used to support either the rice pot or the round-bottomed frying pan above the fire.

This morning's fish stew was hot and spicy. It was made with a fish the men call "gerong," tomatoes, garlic, leeks, very hot chili peppers, sugar, ginger, rock salt, and coconut oil. "Asem" and "keniri," two local fruits unlike anything I know, are combined for a condiment. The stew was delicious, and I asked Sohib, our cook, to taste it. He wasn't insulted and said he could make it too. There's a fresh "gerong" on the *Harini,* and Sohib says he'll make it at our camp tonight.

The five-man dugout I bought in Labuan has been pulled on board the *Harini.* I hope, when we get to the Tjigenter, there's enough water in the river so we can paddle up a way. There are crocodiles—huge ones, I'm told, with bodies thicker than mine—but I'll have to be lucky to see one. If we have the right tide, so that there is enough water in the river, we will paddle upstream as far as we can go. This should provide some new subjects to photograph.

Today is a beautiful day—soft white clouds and not a sign of rain. Ong Tjibun, by the way, has donned Sinaga's belt and sheath knife for the duration of the *Harini* trip, which will take about two and a half more hours. We'll land first on Handeuleum island opposite the Tjigenter's mouth. There are gray monkeys on Handeuleum, which I need, and the fruit bats, which seem to have left Peutjang, may be there too.

Whip snake

There is nothing much to do on the *Harini* but to enjoy the sun, which I am doing bare chested, and to look at a very monotonous coastline—a flat, mostly forested plateau that rises to different heights as it goes away from the shore. The highest point on the peninsula—Pajoeng, it is called—is 480 meters (about 1,600 feet) up, and there are plenty of small hills. Climbing these hills isn't too bad when the foliage is thornless, like the arenga palm and some of the lianas, but otherwise you can't grab anything.

We've just seen Krakatau in the haze ahead of us. It is a perfect volcano shape, like Fuji. Krakatau erupted in 1883, killing hundreds of people; the tidal wave that followed the eruption destroyed the small village of Djung Kulon, on the site of which our tower now stands.

The men are getting ready to troll behind the *Harini.* Watch-

Overleaf:
Trees and rattan

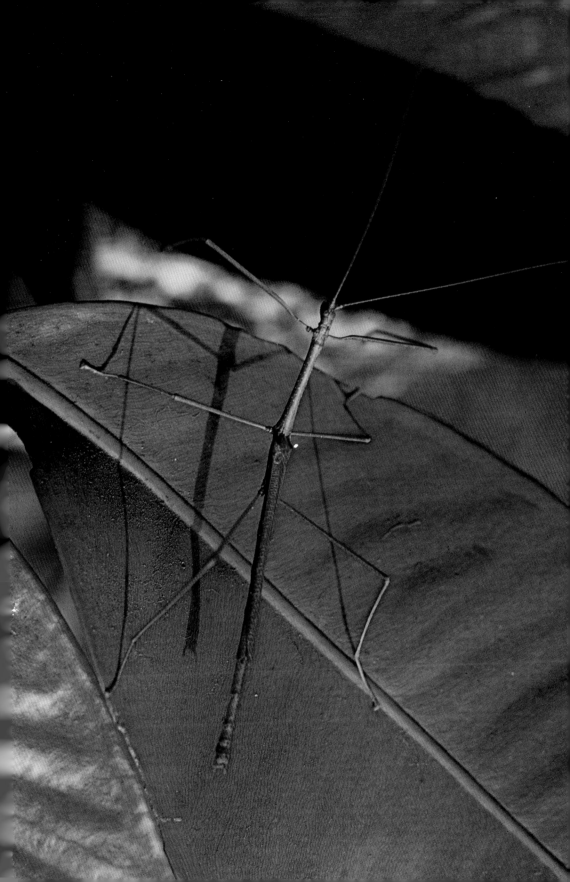

Rhinoceros hornbills
eating figs

Peafowl in palm tre

Monitor lizard

Gray gibbon

ing them reminds me of the time—it was in the 1950s—I made a voyage across the Pacific in a magnificent yacht, the *Varua* (the name means soul in Tahitian). It still belongs to its builder, William Albert Robinson, the man who with a variety of companions—one at a time—sailed around the world in the smallest vessel ever, the *Svap*. He and a Harvard parasitologist, Dr. David Bonnet, and I, aided by two Tahitians, one a cook and the other a seaman, sailed from Samoa to New Guinea in an attempt to trace Polynesian migration routes by taking blood samples from the people on the islands who were thought to be Polynesian even though they lived in Melanesia. There are three major zones in the central Pacific. Polynesia includes Samoa, Hawaii, the Society Islands, the Marquesas, and ethnologically but not geographically, New Zealand; the people are golden brown. Melanesia includes the Solomons and Fijis, New Ireland, New Guinea, the New Hebrides, and New Caledonia; the people are almost black. Micronesia includes the Gilbert Islands, the Marshalls, the Ellice Islands, and the Marianas. Many Polynesians have filariasis, a parasitic disease common in the tropics, and this disease often results in elephantiasis—huge swelling of the legs, the scrotum, and sometimes other parts of the body. Elephantiasis is caused by an obstruction of the lymph channels, and in many cases, the obstruction results from an infestation of the channels by the filariasis parasite. Polynesians have a distinct type of filaria: these worms can be detected in the blood not just at night, when other types of filaria are detectable in the blood, but at all times. Our job in the islands was to take blood samples from the people every three hours for twenty-four hours, and by establishing the daytime presence of filaria, to get evidence of the people's Polynesian heritage. It is not a simple thing to land unannounced on an island and try to get blood. Not at all.

I usually landed first and made a speech in poor pidgin English about what a great man Bonnet was. This sort of thing is usual in the Pacific, where every bigwig has a "talking chief." When I'd finished praising Bonnet he would stick my finger, smear the blood on a slide, and put the slide under a microscope. Everyone brave enough to look was then invited to peer into the microscope and see the things wiggling around on the slide. Three cigarettes could then usually buy one person, then another—and others—to try the new game.

The most difficult thing of all was getting subjects to stay near us for twenty-four hours. A machete, three yards of cloth, and a can of corned beef were the bribes.

It's pretty windy on the *Harini* and difficult to write. I started to write about fishing from the *Varua*. The crew did. Also I saw and photographed a volcano on that trip. So many things

Tjitandahon River meeting the sea

recall that trip. For example, someone is grating coconut meat this morning; one of the things I did on the *Varua* trip was collect small three-legged coconut-grating stools carved by the island people. The islanders sit on these stools and grate the coconut on a projecting end that's made to look like the neck of an animal, tipped with either a serrated shell or a filed piece of tin. The style of the stools is essentially similar from island to island.

August 26, 12:10 P.M.

Really too rough to try to write. Just had lunch—two fillets of "gerong," fried in margarine with onion and garlic. Eaten with cold rice and a cucumber. Good enough. Hunger is the best spice. Cold tea; also, a small banana—we had some brought in from Labuan.

Landing soon.

Sunday, August 27, 3:30 P.M.

I'm in my tent at the mouth of the Tjigenter, trying to rest. But I'm too restless. I can't work any more today, for two reasons. First Sinaga, whose help I need, has a high temperature. There are at least ten infected tick spots on his body. Not getting the head out after a tick is well entrenched is serious. Luckily we had a rendezvous here with the Schenkels, and Mrs. Schenkel gave Sinaga a hypo load of penicillin. She sterilized her gear in a teapot on the open fire, and when I remarked on this, told me that her first case in Udjong Kulon involved lancing an enormous abscess on someone's butt; the abscess developed after a medical aid in Labuan gave the patient an injection with a needle he sterilized once a day.

The second reason I can't work is that my left eye is almost closed. I was stung by a bee this morning. Mrs. Schenkel got the sting out, but that didn't keep the spot from swelling. I just dabbed on some Solarcaine, an ointment used for sunburn and for bites also, so it doesn't hurt, but I've had it since 10 A.M. Everyone thinks I have such a grand time on these excursions.

We put our canoe over the sandbar at high tide last night, so there was enough water for us to go up the river about an hour's paddle. The Schenkels were in another canoe, in front of us. The Tjigenter is not very spectacular, but it's a nice stream, well hemmed in with masses of palm and other trees. When the rocks and shallow water stopped us, the Schenkels, who had often been to the area before, returned while Harum and I walked on, sometimes in the river, sometimes along the banks, which are rather high and covered with bush. It wasn't any different from the survey walk; we even reached the fallen tree on which we'd crossed the Tjigenter on the first day of the survey.

men drag our
ut canoe over a
bar during high
at the mouth of
Tjigenter.

ne-by-twelve-foot
with sewn-in floor
screened windows
es a comfortable
.

There were tiny swallows and some kingfishers, but not to photograph. I did the Schenkel's canoe going up the river, and to give scale to the picture, used Sinaga in front of the Schenkels in our canoe going down. The Schenkels stopped halfway up the river when they saw some rhino tracks. They were barefoot, up to their knees in mud, and were very occupied measuring the exact size of the rhino prints.

Sinaga is resting now.

There was nothing much for lunch today except rice, peanuts, boiled sweet potatoes, and some salt fish. So I opened a can of corned beef and cooked half of it with about four cabbage leaves cut up, a sliced carrot, some diced onion and garlic, salt, pepper, and one small hot red pepper. Not bad with a cold boiled sweet potato as bread. The real treat was a slice of pumpernickel spread with peanut butter and Australian apricot jam and washed down with tea.

August 27, 4:50 P.M.

Rested for almost an hour, but didn't sleep. My air mattress is a very lightweight one, but I've been dissatisfied with it since I saw a German one the Schenkels have. It's almost twice as

Our dugout canoe returns to the mouth of the Tjigenter after exploring upstream.

wide as mine, and instead of having four long lengthwise rolls, as mine does, it is cut up in six-inch squares. Some difference. I fall off mine half the time.

I just gave Sinaga two aspirins. He has a temperature of almost 100°, and Mrs. Schenkel will give him another penicillin shot tomorrow, before we start back to the tower. Tomorrow we'll go to Handeuleum island and see if the monkeys are in a cooperative mood. Enang went looking for fruit bats there while we were upriver, but he didn't find any. So this has not been a very successful sortie, though I do have some fairly good pictures of the river.

Going up by canoe we saw many empty clamshells, but found only three full ones. The clams are large and heavy, and the pigs like them too—and get them. There are also oysters about —good-sized ones. But only the empty shells are to be found. The beach near here is littered with shells. Many of these— cowries, shells from clams of the genus Tridacna, auger shells, spider shells, and shells of several other kinds of snails—familiar to me from the Society Islands.

The tide goes up the Tjigenter several miles, and the water is very brackish or slightly so, depending on the tide. There is no bore, a rapid tidal flow that often builds up where the tide comes back to the sea; the river here is hardly large enough to accommodate one. It was a tidal bore that swamped Michael Rockefeller's canoe in the Eilanden river in West Irian in 1963.

The Schenkels examine and measure rhinoceros footprints in the mud at the edge of the Tjigenter.

Monday, August 28, 1:45 P.M.
Back on the *Harini,* heading for the tower.
This morning Harum and I tried the river again—just the two

of us, though he doesn't speak a word of English and I certainly speak no Sundanese. I was after a fabulous-looking stork-billed kingfisher which works this part of the river. We spent two hours paddling and drifting silently but had only one fleeting glimpse of him, not enough to photograph. I once wanted to be able to take pictures as easily and as quickly as I could see. This wouldn't be good enough here; here you need telescopic vision as well.

When Harum and I got back to the mouth of the river, Sinaga had broken camp, and most of the gear was already on the *Harini*.

My eye is still slightly closed. More unpleasant, I found an enormous tick this morning, embedded in my scrotal sac. I managed to extract it without breaking off its head. Then I painted the area with Merthiolate. Very attractive.

We landed at Handeuleum about 11 A.M., and I gave those monkeys a good two hours to show up for the fine banana feast I'd set out for them. But they weren't having any. So back to the *Harini* and "home."

The net aboard is torn—a really large tear—and there has been no fishing. I opened a can of corned beef for lunch and ate it cold—part of it with a cucumber and a small red onion. After that, the big treat: a slice of pumpernickel with peanut butter and jam, and cold tea. Canned or not, this bread, Funke's Real Dutch Pumpernickel (8-oz.; manufactured by Funke's, Haarlem, Holland; est. Holland; 1834, and purveyor to H.M. Queen of the Netherlands), deserves a gold medal. It comes sliced, with the slices about the same size as those of the thin-sliced packaged pumpernickels sold in New York groceries. I must find out who carries it in New York City.

I'm a little let down now. Two and a half days shot to hell for some river pictures that are good, but not worth it. Not an animal; not even a bird. Correction; I did get some snaps of a fish hawk overhead, which probably won't be worth publishing, and some of a long yellow-tailed squirrel, typically hidden by the heavy foliage—great shots of his tail. I wonder if I'll have to face the fact that I may have to do some of these animals in a camouflaged setup in the Djakarta zoo? I can't stay here forever.

It isn't that I'm tired or bored. But when I left New York, the projected closing date for this issue was November 1. I've asked Pat Hunt to let me know how long I actually have. I reached Udjong Kulon August 6 and didn't get set for a day or two, so I've really had only a scant three weeks of shooting so far. Not very much when you consider I'm doing a wilderness, and with no communication to the outside.

The Schenkels leave for their monthly getaway to Bogor early

Thursday morning. They're coming over to the tower for dinner Wednesday and will pick up my film—Take 2—and the mail I am sending. They'll give it to Amir Daud, the *Time-Life* stringer in Djakarta; and he'll ship it to New York. When the Schenkels come back, September 6, they'll bring any cables or mail Daud gives them for me. The next boat to Labuan is about the 15th, and Daud is to send a car to meet it. The logistics are enormous.

Tuesday, August 29, 7:30 A.M.

A cloudy morning, but no rain during the night. There was lots of wind though. I thought the roof was coming off. Metal pieces form the junctions of the four-sided tile roof, which pitches to a point. The metal is loose, and the pieces—and tiles too—bang around something fierce. I woke up twice.

Just now a small lizard, a gecko—if not a gecko, similar to one—is up and sounding off. It is a two-syllable exclamation.

I removed another tick this morning, from my left shin. Unfortunately he was too far in to get out whole, so his head is still in my shin, and I'll have to wait for developments. The spot itches like hell, probably psychologically, but maybe not, since it was itching that drew my attention to it in the first place.

Tomorrow I'll be going out to the new blind made especially for the magnificent peacock I saw last Friday. He seems to be of a species that's larger and more brightly colored than the one that's domesticated in America. The male crest is different too.

I saw him again late yesterday afternoon, but the sun was almost gone by then, and except briefly—when he came near a tree and I used a branch as an arch over his head—before that he was against an uninteresting background. I want him from ground level.

Some of the men are going over to Peutjang island today to build a blind from which I can try for some decent stuff on the rusa.

I must spend an hour now cleaning my cameras and lenses. It's so dry here now that the air is full of bits of leaves and dust. Also, the ground is covered with layers of brown leaves—something I don't like with snakes around. This morning I cleared the path to my outdoor john, about a hundred feet from the tower and hidden under a tree. I go down sometimes in low slippers and I want to see the clear ground. One of the few things I forgot to bring to Java was chloride of lime, to disinfect a latrine; I remembered it in Djakarta, but couldn't find any there. The list of things to take on a jungle trip is unending, and I don't even have a checklist, which is stupid—but one's requirements always vary so. If I can find time, I may try to make a list of what was needed on this trip. No one will believe it.

The big peacock just came by the tower and is now (according to the distance scale on the 1000mm lens) 220 feet from my window. He headed for the "sempur" tree, then turned. Too bad. It would have made a nice photographic relationship, but anyway, there's not a drop of sun, which means no brilliance on the plumage.

He's ducked into the bushes now. Very cloudy but I'm sure it will be sunny in a moment.

Now the sun is out and against me. It would make beautiful back lighting. So where is my peacock? Completely hidden in the bushes, that's where. This is what is known as luck. Bad luck.

Now the orange-bellied flower-peckers are back again in front of the tower. They seem to be crazy about the cherry-sized fruit on the purple-flowering bushes out front.

Lucky enough to get a few shots of the bird as the sun darted in and out. One shows him feeding on a twig, which also had a blossom; you can see the purple fruit in his beak—at least I hope so, because I saw it in the Nikon, and usually what I see, I get. A lot of wind, a slow F11 lens, and 20X magnification are not ideal for photography.

An orange-bellied flower-pecker eats the purple fruit on the bushes in front of the tower.

Now there's another bird, with rather dull plumage. He's light brown, somewhat darker than a cedar waxwing, but about the same size, and he has an undulating flight. I'm using him to practice on—for the other beauty. You have to be fast, really fast. By the time you find the bird in the camera and then get the right focus, the bird is very often gone.

While all this has been going on, I've been putting some "tongkol" (the fish that reminds me of a bonito or an albacore) together with some leeks and carrots. The mixture is now starting to simmer. I'm keeping one eye on it and watching the field with the other.

Among the creatures I'm after is an enormous bumblebee—or a cousin of one. But none has appeared this morning. The bees are so large that at first I thought they were hummingbirds.

Before lunch I set the Polaroid for Sinaga and had him take some snaps of my window setup. The 500 and 1000mm lenses, tripods, and my table are in the foreground. You can also see a lamp with a big white shade. It burns kerosene, gives about as much light as a 100- or a 150-watt bulb, and was made in Red China. Next to it the American lamps I brought to Java with me look like candles. The *Harini* has one of these lamps, and as soon as I saw it I asked Talbot to send me one from Djakarta when he went back. If this is trading with China, so be it.

August 29, 1:15 P.M.

After Sinaga finished the Polaroids I spent an hour, and a roll and a half of Kodachrome, doing close-ups of the purple flowers on the bushes out front. These blossoms attract ants, and also, a kind of black iridescent flying insect the size of a small bee. I concentrated on a single five-petaled blossom. At first I merely wanted an identifying shot of it, but then I realized there was great beauty in its form and color, in its placement in the surrounding buds and leaves, and also in the insects that come to light on it. So I really went to work on it.

Meanwhile Sohib was boiling some potatoes to eat with the "tongkol." The fish was caught Saturday, three days ago, from the *Harini,* and when we got back to the tower yesterday I put some fillets in the refrigerator to keep.

The fish-leek-and-carrot mixture turned out quite well. With it I had two small boiled potatoes, and on them some drawn butter. I bought two pounds of butter in Djakarta and have been guarding it for special meals—and this lunch turned out to be special enough to merit not only the butter but also two glasses of Chablis.

I'm saving one big slice of the fish, already cooked, and some broth and will try to do it au gratin with noodles, the same way chicken or turkey Tetrazzini is done. On the *Varua* I used to do dolphin—not porpoise, but the "mahi-mahi" of the Polynesians—this way; I called it Mahi Mahi Tetrazzini. Lesson learned on the *Varua* and elsewhere: make the most of what you've got. I'm certainly making the most of what food there is in Udjong Kulon.

Luckily, among the things I've got here are three (there were five) small cans of Brie cheese I bought in the Paris airport en route. I'll serve one to the Schenkels when they come to dinner tomorrow. The main course will be chicken in the pot. The two chickens for it were caught early this morning, for that is the only time you can get hold of the chickens here. Since Talbot sent me two jars of Danish shrimp, I may do a shrimp omelet to start the dinner with. For dessert, bananas fried in margarine, with honey.

I hope the pictures I'm doing here turn out as well as most of my culinary projects have. Not that I haven't lived, and wouldn't live again on tomato herring to do a good story. Food doesn't replace sex, but it sure helps.

August 29, 2:45 P.M.

Just did a magnificent stork-billed kingfisher on a bush about sixty feet from my window. His tail was hidden in the first shots,

A stork-billed king-fisher photographed with a 1000mm mirror lens from a window in the tower.

but then he turned before flying away. It was the same species I tried so hard for in the Tjigenter, with no luck there.

I'm working at the tower window so I can wait for the monitor lizard, who comes from behind the tower to the west; I've put out some fish for him to keep him coming. From where I am I can also watch for any animals who come into the field in front.

Thursday, August 31, 9:15 A.M.

The *Badak* left early this morning. The next time out for it will be the 19th (four days later than I thought it would be leaving), to buy supplies for both camps—mine and the Schenkels'. Since a car will come from Djakarta to meet it, I may go out for a three-day breather—and also to check the Djakarta zoo. Either the *Badak* will wait or I'll have the *Harini* come up to stand by.

The *Badak* is part of a grant from the World Wildlife Fund, which is working to encourage wildlife research. So are all the Schenkels' expenses. After six months here the Schenkels will go back to Basle. So far, they haven't had much luck photographically. In the beginning, when it was wet, they tracked about a half-dozen rhinos, and Dr. Schenkel was able to observe one for about an hour. It was so hidden by foliage that he couldn't get any clear pictures; but then, he's studying rhino behavior—territory, feeding habits, etc.—and only incidentally trying to get photos.

When the Schenkels came to dinner last night they brought Djuhari, the warden in charge of Udjong Kulon. I'd asked Sinaga. So we were five.

I tried to do a good dinner. First, some of the Italian salami I received from Joan, my former wife, before I left. (It's a real long one, and I still have more than half of it.) Then a dish prepared by Sohib from the two different kinds of crab, one with beautiful red spots on its shell (I photographed it on the beach before it went into Sohib's pot), and a single small crayfish exactly like the South African ones we buy for the tails; these were all cooked together in a yellowish broth, Indonesian style. (I'll watch how Sohib does it the next time, though I love crab just plain steamed, like lobster with drawn butter.) Digression re Sohib and shellfish: the three large clams we took out of the Tjigenter Sunday were cooked by him with diced potatoes, and if I didn't know better, I'd say someone showed him a version of Manhattan clam chowder.

The next course Wednesday was a beautiful fish, a "talang." This fish is about as long as, but somewhat wider than a bluefish, and has yellow streaks on its belly and lower head; a serrated set of long fins runs from its middle (I think pectoral) fin

115

to the tail, both top and bottom. Nice white flesh. A little bony maybe—but I've shown Sohib how to fillet a fish; he uses the head and bones for his own cooking. We get quite enough fish now from the *Harini*, which sets a net every night.

The biggest dish was chicken in the pot. I had two chickens, which were caught Tuesday, killed yesterday morning, and I boiled them gently for an hour in water with salt and pepper. Then I added some finely diced leeks (found in Labuan), some small onions, and four sliced carrots. The birds were so tough that if I'd started with the vegetables, the vegetable would have been mush by the time the chicken was tender. All of these dishes were eaten with cold steamed rice, Indonesian style. I even had a little Major Grey's Chutney to go with the chicken, and a salad of sliced canned beets and fresh cucumber, served with a dressing of olive oil, ReaLemon, vinegar, and garlic.

Dessert was fried plantains drenched in honey. Then came the cheese, with pumpernickel and butter. Later Mrs. Schenkel had at least a dozen of my precious *hopje* candies.

Right now I'm waiting for my monster—the monitor lizard —to come out of the forest. He always emerges from beneath or over a fallen tree. Yesterday morning he came, grabbed a

An orange crab with red spots crawls along the shore at the mouth of the Tjidaon.

nice piece of fish, and left immediately—before I could get a picture.

I've done something different today. One of the men speared an eagle ray two nights ago, and yesterday afternoon I let it hang in the sun—with the wind toward the lizard's lair. I made up several nice pieces of the very bony and tough meat from the head. Then I had Harum drive three small wooden stakes into the ground and fasten the fish to the stakes with tough vine cord, which you can't see. If the monster wants this meal he's going to have to eat some of it in front of two cameras now set behind a palm blind.

One camera is loaded with Kodachrome II, and the other with high-speed Ektachrome. The two films have very different color qualities, and I like the security of two different cameras, two different lenses, and two different films. If any of the film is ruined in processing, it won't be the first time this has happened to color film; since *Life* does the Ektachrome, and Kodak the Kodachrome, I should be safe. The Kodachrome is infinitely superior in color contrast and grain, but sometimes the high-speed Ektachrome gives you a desirable muted look.

I thought Amir, who's watching for the lizard from the tower, threw a pebble over here a second ago. But it was just another piece of old tile falling from the tower's roof. It blew so hard last night I thought the whole thing was coming down. If I can't get someone to climb it and do some repairs, I'll have to move to the tent to get some sleep.

Tomorrow I'm going to spend the whole day in the Peutjang rusa blind. Then, on Saturday, we—I and all but two of the men —push out for a four-day sortie on which we'll go clear around the tip of the peninsula. I'm working on a map that will show all the sorties. The *Harini* will take us to the neck of the sanctuary on the north coast, where the water is calmer than it is along the south coast. Here we'll land and cut our own path across the neck of the sanctuary to a point on the south coast where there's a warden's station. At this point, which is called Karangrandjang, we'll establish a minor headquarters and spend the first night. The second day we'll walk along the beach about twelve kilometers, to the mouth of the Tjikevsik. We'll camp there—I'll just use tarps, no tent—then return to base the next day. The fourth day we'll recross the isthmus and reboard the *Harini,* which will be waiting to take us back to the tower.

I'm taking Amir along on this sortie. He needs to see what we are doing. Also, the trip will be good experience for him.

The two men who are remaining at the tower will sleep under it and never allow it to be unattended. There's a gang of bush cutters working not far away (for the Schenkels). And yesterday a launch landed some army people whom I suspect have been poaching here when no one's around; they have the guns. Also, because it's now so incredibly dry, I worry about fire. I have a large heap of beach sand under the tower and a box of sand upstairs to stop a kerosene or gasoline fire from a lamp or stove; I've also had the men clear away the enormous quantities of dead leaves that were around the tower.

It's 10 A.M., and the monitor still hasn't arrived for his feast. The sun is right on the bait.

Yesterday I worked the new peacock blind, and it was perfect. I was right about the male's territory. He came all around me, part of the time with a female. Using a huge telephoto lens, I couldn't keep both of the birds in focus unless they were rather close together. At first, they weren't, but they obliged just before the sun faded out.

It was so windy that every time the poor male tried to show off his great tail—part of the peacock's courting—a gust of wind would swing him clear around. I hope I have some pictures of this.

10:40 A.M. Well, I got him—the monitor, that is. He came to the bait, and as hard as he tried, couldn't tear the eagle ray meat loose. I wish I had movies of it: his whole huge ugly body digging in with effort and his great tail swishing around as he tried to tear off the meat.

I got him on two of the baited stakes, but he left the third, the nearest one. I hope he'll come back to this later because I'd love an extreme close-up with the 1000mm. He already filled the frame but I'd like a full-length shot showing the whole monster —he is a monster—from the top of his head to his dainty claws, and with that enormous black tongue flicking out.

A peacock displaying his tail to a peahen was blown over moments later by a high wind.

The lizard hasn't been back for the last piece of fish. Maybe he's not hungry enough. Yesterday he arrived with a white chicken feather stuck to the side of his mouth, and it had been days since we threw what was left of that dead chicken into downwind.

I've been napping, because of no sleep last night. The tower roof is fixed now. The men opened up some tiles from below, crawled up and out, and nailed the tin down again.

I had a half-hour lie-down on a mat in the sun, then a fifty-yard swim before lunch. My waistline is down two belt holes; that's about two inches, and all to the good.

Two peahens are in the field in front of me. I'm at the tower window, watching. A few minutes ago I read a little of Robert Ruark's *Honey Badger*. It's not the powerhouse *Uhuru* was, but interesting to the African fraternity.

The idea of a list of what I brought here still fascinates me. There is always one haversack, the kind you sling over your shoulder; mine dates from World War II—the North American campaign—and came from Abercrombie and Fitch. It is still solid, albeit dirty. I call it my war bag, and it has gone to Africa, to New Guinea, and on every bush trip I've ever made. It contains:

The monitor lizard cannot remove fish meat that has been fastened to a stake.

1. A small kerosene Primus stove in its own tin box. (You can find kerosene everywhere in the world because it's what's used for wick lamps.)
2. My old Boy Scout mess kit in a canvas case. Folding frying pan, tiny pot, a plate, and a cup. With the mess kit, a magnificent steel gadget consisting of a can opener,

knife, fork, and spoon that nest together. This has a swastika on it, which isn't surprising, since I took the gadget from a burned out German tank at El Guettar. There's a cheap copy of it made now.

3. A flat one-quart canteen.
4. A cot-sized mosquito net with nylon strings to hang it from.

Dammit! Two gray monkeys just went by, but too far to the left for me to get them. I caught sight of them with a sort of perimeter vision, for although my eyes are only 20–40 without glasses, I do spot any movement, almost to 180 degrees. Talbot has fantastic eyesight—double length—and he's as good at spotting things as Harum, who often stops on the trail ahead of me, freezing like a bird dog at the sight of an animal that for the life of me I can't see at all until it moves again.

I may have to build another blind, in left field. I now have three blinds here: the big one built two weeks ago at center field; the one built for the peacock at first base; and the new one, for the lizard, at home plate.

5. A sewing kit that includes a stitching awl and waxed thread; also, patches and glue for the air mattress.
6. A first-aid kit, including a snakebite outfit. The kit varies in size from expedition to expedition. For Java, I brought everything: Achromycin, aspirin, codeine, Miltown, Halazone (purifies any water), Mercurochrome and Merthiolate, thermometers, forceps, needles, surgical floss, bandages, swabs, tapes, sprain bandages, Band-Aids (most essential), gauze pads, ointments and salves, sunburn lotion, Alka-Seltzer and Bisodol (for results of my own cooking), Lomotil and paregoric (for diarrhea), antimalaria pills, potassium permanganate. One thing I haven't got, because I forgot about it, is enough Roche's Valium. Robert Ardrey introduced me to this this spring on my way to the Congo. It seems to relax your intellect in a somewhat different way than Miltown does; anyhow, while you're tossing around in bed, you stop asking yourself questions like, "Did I get him in focus?" and "Will I ever get a rhino?" I have a few pills left and should have brought more. The whole medical kit doesn't always go into the war bag. Just Halazone, Mercurochrome, Band-Aids, antibiotic salve, aspirins, and the snakebite outfit. The rest goes with my clothing and other gear.
7. A small bug bomb and its companion, a small bottle of insect repellent; a two-cell flashlight with two extra batteries; and a half-roll of toilet paper. A full roll is

too large to include in the bag. I never, never go anywhere except East Hampton without No. 7.

8. A fairly large and heavy Sheffield steel sheath knife,
which can double as a machete or a small ax. A tiny
Carborundum stone for the knife and a tiny can of ma-
chine oil for the stone (and for guns).

9. A thin nylon cord that will support a man.

10. Fishhooks of different sizes and a monofilament line.

11. Sometimes the Walther .765, with extra rounds, and
also, its cleaning rod and patches.

12. A pint flask for whisky.

13. A Boy Scout-type knife and an army marching compass, both on lanyards and worn on the person during
marches; a waterproof matchcase; and an Abercrombie
and Fitch altimeter.

14. Tiny five-power Japanese Nikon binoculars, which
weigh no more than book-author-type horn-rimmed
glasses. I also have ten-power binoculars with me,
but I don't carry them in the war bag because they're
too tricky to spot with—the game, particularly if it's a
bird, is sometimes gone before you find it.

15. In cold climates, I manage to stuff in a knitted helmet,
some wind goggles, and a pair of gloves. I also have
army-flyer-type sunglasses.

There must be more, which will occur later. The gear is out of
the bag now, and I don't see anything else. Just remembered:

16. Sometimes a thick candle.

17. Sometimes a steel mirror for signaling.

For clothing on this trip, my basic outfit:

1. Three pairs of khaki trousers without cuffs (they catch
in everything and you can't tuck them into socks).

2. Three long-sleeved khaki shirts, three T-shirts, and
three pairs of boxer shorts. Six handkerchiefs (I'm using
colorful Western-type ones here, because they're large
enough to fit well under the neck of a shirt and keep
ticks from crawling in).

3. Three pairs of reinforced athletic hose—normal length;
one longer pair for tucking in trousers.

4. An old pair of bird-shooter boots, half-leg high for
maximum support and snakebite prevention; a pair of
Marine-issue reverse leather boots, ankle high (no
desert boots, which wouldn't last two weeks on coral
rocks, mud, etc.); a pair of khaki basketball-type sneakers (from L. L. Bean), which has proved great. The
sneakers dry out quickly (far more quickly than leather

footgear would) after wet-foot landing from the canoe to the beach. Happens all the time. Also, sometimes you just have to cross a shallow river or a swamp. Another thing to the sneakers' credit: good rubber bottoms, thick enough to stop most thorns. But not all of them—I've pulled plenty out of my feet. The lower stem of the "salah" palm here is so thickly studded with solid two-inch thorns you can hardly see it. If you step on one of these thorns, which are often hiding below dead leaves, you're really stepping on something. When your feet stop missing those thorns, and get you fouled up in roots all the time, it's past the hour when you should be marching here; you need a rest, and as soon as you can get it.

5. A denim jacket and a sweater (I have yet to wear either of these here, where it's cold in the middle of the night, but not before). A plastic raincoat and a matching hat. Also a lightweight brimmed all-around hat (from Lock's in London) and an Israeli army hat. A pair of slippers and a Japanese cotton robe.

I also have two large towels, an air mattress, sleeping bag, air pillow, two sheets, a lightweight cotton blanket, and two pillowcases.

Just remembered I didn't list my toilet kit for the war bag. Also in it are a bar of soap in a plastic case, and a can of flea powder. (I'm allergic to flea bites.) And something I forgot to list with the contents of the medical kit; some antibacterial, antilouse soap.

3:15 P.M. It's time I went to the blind and made a living. No writing there this time. *Extreme* vigilance.

August 31, 5:05 P.M.

Just back—back in the tower, that is. Went to the first-base blind instead of the large one because Mr. Peacock was there. Didn't take any shots of him though. He wasn't close enough, or in the right situation. Now that I have basic material on him, I'm looking for an especially beautiful tree or branch behind him, or his bright head outlined against black or dark brown. I don't have too much high-speed Ektachrome left, and I must use what I have with the 1000mm lens—hopefully for rusa or rhino rather than repeat shots of the peacock. I also want other game—particularly giant hornbills and macaques.

Tomorrow I'll sit all day in the Peutjang blind, hoping for rusa. I wish I could describe what it means to sit in a blind, peering through cracks in the palm weave, watching for a movement. Then seeing a bird or an animal. Getting it and the camera lined up like aiming a rifle. Moving the camera, mounted on a heavy tripod, slowly with the animal, focusing all the time, because the animal's distance keeps changing. The light is changing too—a cloud, the shadow of a tree. No time to measure; you must guess the change. Then deciding when to click. If you're too early, the head or something else isn't right. If the animal's moving too fast for your lens and exposure, then you don't shoot, because even if you are lucky and do get an interesting blur, interesting blurs are old hat now.

The concentration on just a few minutes' shooting is fantastic and nerve-racking. I wish I had faster perception on focusing. My reflexes are great, but my eyes could be better—sharper, that is. Experience helps a lot, anticipating the next move, talking to yourself, to the animal, too, saying, "Please lift your head," "Don't move"—many crazy things. Such a contrast to the photography I did for a Japanese cookbook some years ago: nice, dead fish artfully arranged at the edge of a temple, etc. I like doing both kinds of assignments. But physically this Java job is about as trying as an assignment can be. Maybe it's not as bad as the "Nine Worst Days in My Life," which were spent climbing the Ruwenzori, but on that job I did only landscapes, nothing moving. What bothers me here enormously is that I'm taking photographic gambles every day and can't check the results. I sent Take 2 off today—forty-two rolls. I may hear about them in about three weeks.

I bought six cans of tomato juice in Djakarta. They're reserved strictly for "Bloodies," as Joan calls them—and today I need one. Cheers!

August 31, 6:45 P.M.

It is now all of a quarter to seven, and the day is done, finished. I've had dinner. Soon I'm going to open a small jar of native raspberry jam Elin bought for me at the July Fourth fair in Vinalhaven. I still have a small jar of wild strawberry jam that my neighbors Bo and Austin Lamont gave me, but I'm such a miser. The jams are like gold.

I'll try to read *Honey Badger* before going to sleep. Probably before 7:30—and up at about 5:30. But I rarely sleep through the night. Maybe I will tonight. With the roof fixed, it should be quiet.

August 31, 7:20 P.M.

Not sure about going to bed at all now—not after what just happened.

I was sitting at this table writing. A movement caught my eye, and I glanced up. About eighteen inches from me was the head of a bright green snake, on the outside window sill. He was motionless for a moment. Then, crawling along—all six feet of him (I measured the space he occupied later)—he

123

started to come toward the open window (broken out long ago).

I stood up, very slow, waited a minute, then ever so slowly and carefully raised and fastened the palm curtain that might block the snake's progress through the window. Next, I ran into the storeroom and emptied the largest carton there. Then I found a stick.

By now the snake was halfway past the window. I waited for him. He came a little farther. Then, using the stick, I dumped him into the box.

But he was too long, and before I could close the box covers with the stick, he came right out again—at me. I was wearing slippers and shorts, not very good snake gear. Since I wasn't equipped for snake handling I scampered up onto the seat of my chair. I should have improvised a noose at the end of the stick, but it was all too fast.

I called to Amir and Sohib, who were supposed to be below. No answer. They were AWOL at the beach, having a gabfest. Meanwhile the snake glided under my bed. I got down from the chair and closed the doors, thinking he would stay. Then I ran outside and down to the beach for help. I really wanted to capture that snake. He was a beautiful brilliant green, like the American grass snake, which I hoped he was as harmless as.

Anyway, he was gone when the troop—Amir, Sohib, and I— arrived.

Last year, on the Serengeti plains, I captured a huge puff adder. I had gone into the bathroom hut to wash my hands, opened the door against the tub, and left the door open while I washed. When I walked out again, I'd closed the door after me. The next visitor had opened the same door, seen a huge puff adder, and screamed for help. I ran back, and he and I managed to get the adder into a cardboard carton, in which I kept him until the next morning for filming. Then I let him loose.

The green snake tonight was a hundred times more agile and lithe than the adder. No pictures, alas!

Friday, September 1, 7 A.M.

I didn't sleep too well last night, after the snake. Left a small hurricane lamp burning with a very low wick when I went to bed. As a result, was able to see a mouse—maybe it was a young rat—scamper out of the storeroom. Probably just the kind of thing the snake would have liked.

The floor under my bed has enough holes and enough large gaps between the boards to let many snakes escape or enter.

Last night Sohib came in with his big golok, the local machete, and did not understand why I didn't want him to kill the snake. In all my travels I have killed only one snake—and that one, a good-sized cobra, I really had to kill. The cobra (this happened in the ex-Belgian Congo, in 1951) had climbed up to the ridgepole in a cook tent, and it was either get rid of him or sacrifice the cook. I thought the snake might be a spitting cobra. These creatures forcibly spit out their venom, which can cover quite a distance. So I put on my glasses before I tried to shoot it down with a pistol. I fired two shots, and both missed. Finally the cook, responding to my sign language, knocked the snake down with a long stick, and I poured a kettle of boiling water over it as it landed on the ground. Killed and cooked at once! But I didn't try to eat it nor have I ever tried to eat any of the canned rattlesnake sold in the U.S.

Had a little trouble with Sohib this morning. I'd given him two duck eggs and a dish with a couple of spoonfuls of evaporated milk and some salt in it, then left him alone to make an omelet for my breakfast. For some reason—perhaps because out of the corner of my eye I saw him stoop to the ground—I turned back to watch him. From the ground, he picked up the filthiest rag you ever saw, and with this rag he calmly proceeded to wipe the spatula. Hanging near him was the beautiful towel,

The author tastes fish cooked by Sohib in the outdoor kitchen under the tower.

changed every two days, meant for such purposes. No wonder I have a slight diarrhea today. It's a wonder I don't have a proper case of dysentery. He's supposed to boil all the water he uses, even that for cooking. What this boiled water tastes like straight—with the nasty flavor of the fire smoke, plus that of some salt left by the Indian Ocean in the Tjidaon, from which our water's drawn—even Scotch or bourbon can't disguise; Rose's Lime Cordial does the best by it.

Couldn't get any news out of the *Voice of America,* Philippines, at 6:30 or at 7:00. Nice jazz when I want news.

September 1, 10:15 A.M.

Reached the Peutjang blind at 9:30 after crossing over in the *Harini.* I'm sorry I let Sinaga supervise the site of the blind. It's too close to several wide-buttressed trees, which obstruct the view. Also, it's right on top of one of the most beautiful vine-draped trees around (of course it would have been almost a miracle to get both a tree like that and a rusa in one shot).

In the blind, which is a fairly large one, I have my folding camouflaged stool and a pandanus mat. The mat, which meas-

Harum watches for rusa deer from the blind built in the stags' territory on Peutjang Island.

126

ures about three by five feet, was made in western Java, and I bought it for about $1 (it would have cost $10 in Tahiti or Samoa). They used to make pandanus sleeping mats in Hawaii; in the old days, wealthy Hawaiians piled them a foot or two high to make a very nice bed.

Harum is watching through a porthole in one side of the blind, I'm at the other—though I doubt if any deer will come downwind. While waiting, I'm checking my underwater gear, because if it's not windy, I may have a go at the coral reef right off the Peutjang shore.

Charles Lindbergh was thrilled by what he saw there. I have light sneakers, a face plate, a snorkel, and underwater camera.

I'm afraid that anyone reading this diary will think I'm making an overinterest in food substitute for other things. Could be. Anyhow, it's only 10:20 and I'm eyeing my lunch bag. I saved the livers of the two chickens that went into the main dish for the Schenkel party; then—you guessed it—I chopped them together with a hard boiled egg and some onion, and added mayonnaise. I have two slices of pumpernickel and a flask with about a half pint of red wine; also, a cucumber and some raisins. Yet I've lost in the neighborhood of seven to ten pounds, as my belt has come in two full notches. Trouble is I put the weight back on again so fast when I get out.

André Gide wrote in his book *Voyage au Congo,* "We are doing our best not to find the river boring." I remembered this just now because sitting in a blind all day—once you've seen the trees and vines, that is—can also be boring. Very boring. As a rule I have less patience (especially with stupidity) than anyone I know, but I've spent hours on end in these blinds, often sitting cross-legged, like a Buddha, and almost always keeping very, very quiet.

September 1, 1 P.M.

A female rusa, but too far away and too covered by foliage to get even one shot. Four pigs earlier. No good—too much contrast in lighting, with some very dark areas and some of bright sun.

This is really tiresome. The tower blinds are more open, and you can at least see things move. Here all you see is leaves— and in bad light. Afraid I'll run out of books. Stupidly I didn't bring enough from New York; I thought I'd get a stack of those wonderful Penguins in London, but I never got around to it. Tragic. Have read *Catherine the Great* by Zoé Oldenbourg; very engrossing. Now I'm on Ruark's *Honey Badger,* most of which is interesting. Have a Margery Allingham, which I'm hoarding. On impulse I took Saul Bellow's *Herzog* from New York, but I couldn't read it once before, so I know I won't get through it easily. In 1947 I took *War and Peace* and Nehru's *Glimpses of World History* to Africa and they kept me quite busy. Nehru's book, which is made of letters about world history which he wrote to his daughter while he was in prison, and without any reference material, is probably one of the greatest intellectual virtuoso feats of our time. It also revealed world history as it's seen from the opposite part of the globe.

3:00 P.M. Bingo! First a full-grown rusa stag; then a younger one. In two shots I even got a small gray monkey scampering on a log in the background. The log and the monkey were out of focus. But who cares? I just hope the deer are sharp.

I worked with the big rusa for almost an hour, during which my eyes began to hurt and I developed an excrutiating pain in the back of my neck as I moved my cameras to track him through the branches and constantly adjusted to compensate for abrupt changes of light caused by the wind motion through the trees. Sometimes so dark—1/30 second at F4.5 on the 300, a very handy lens coupled to the exposure meter in the Fotomic.

Rusa stag photographed with a 300mm lens on High Speed Ektachrome at 1/30 of a second at F4.5.

You can focus and adjust exposure from the camera viewer. Had to switch to the 500 in order to get other material more out-of-focus so you could see the deer.

Enang blew the deer session by arriving and scaring all the animals in the region. He misunderstood my instructions—given in Indonesian, yet—and didn't come right back after going to the shore. The rusas showed up while Enang was gone. Had Enang come back later, it wouldn't have been so bad; any earlier and I would have killed him.

I think I have one great shot: the big rusa, head lifted, body partly hidden by a huge tree trunk, and behind him, another buttressed tree. It's all worthwhile now. But I need more even light.

Oddly enough, the wind was exactly from the blind to the deer. (There's a small wind vane—with a prop made from palm leaves—sitting outside the blind, where we can see it from inside.) The big stag did smell us—he kept lifting his head and sniffing—but the smell wasn't strong enough (or the right kind) to alarm him.

I had two metal tripods going—one for a Nikon with the 300mm lens, and the other for a Nikon with the 500mm. Keeping the metal legs from clanking was something. I may have to muffle them.

Another thing: the big male didn't bother to run off the intruder. Yet I'm pretty sure it is his territory. That is why I had the blind built here. I wish Bob Ardrey was here for a few weeks. He was a wonderful companion on the Serengeti plains last year.

The closest the big stag came was about seventy-five feet; generally, he was between one hundred and three hundred feet away. I kept hoping he'd come closer into the clear. I once built a moose blind in northern Minnesota; sunk below the ground, it was right in the moose's path. I was sitting in this pit with a lacework of twigs over me when Mr. Moose suddenly made a beeline for it. I was forced to stand up and scream, which was the simplest way to avoid being accidentally trampled.

I'm now planning not to have the rhino blind, which hasn't been built yet, on the ground. Instead, I want it at least six feet above the ground, and on very stout logs.

Saturday, September 2, 11:30 A.M.

On the *Harini* heading southeast, right into a very strong wind. Whitecaps all over the bright green sea.

Before we rounded the northern corner of the peninsula, the wind was offshore. The spray from the big waves that broke on the beach was lifted into a misty veil over the cresting waves, and when seen against the dark trees marching up to the hills just beyond, looked even flimsier. I made quite a few pictures of this. Photographs of surf seen from the beach are rather common, but this is quite different and could be an introductory shot for the story of Udjong Kulon—a peninsula sticking out into the sea.

Almost too rough to write now. Will try anyway.

We left for the four-day sortie at 9:15 this morning. Today the *Harini* will drop us at the mouth of a river, the Tjisimpang, just opposite the narrow neck of the isthmus (the peninsula swells out and could almost be an island). Then we'll cut our way to the south coast. We could never land there. Huge surf breaking on coral all the time. We'll camp near the Karangrandjang warden's station tonight. Tomorrow we'll walk about twelve kilometers on the beach, to the mouth of the Tjikevsik, and camp there.

Naturally I'll photograph as we go. This is said to be an endless beach of sand with big surf. So I should get some good shots.

The third day, back to Karangrandjang, and the fourth day, north to the other coast, where the *Harini* will be waiting to take us back to headquarters.

Sunday, September 3, 7 A.M.

A lot has happened since yesterday's notes. The landing yesterday proved to be a minor disaster. First of all, it was extreme low tide, so the *Harini* had to stop about a quarter of a mile offshore. Then the canoe couldn't make it much closer.

I put on my gum boots, which are just below knee high, and thought nothing of wading ashore. What I didn't know was that I'd be wading through the worst and deepest mudhole in Udjong Kulon. The mud flats were endless, and not so flat. What started as ankle deep, at the edge of the reef, got to be knee high, then higher. The men, laden with forty-pound loads, were having a hell of a time getting to solid ground. So was I. It would have been dirty but okay, but a magnificent reef heron decided to land about a hundred yards from me, and once he landed, he started fishing. I needed that picture.

Harum was behind me. I motioned to him, holding up five fingers. This means the 500mm lens. He carries that and the 1000mm in two separate leather cases, instantly available. Ten finger means the 1000. He ploughed his way up to me. By then I'd already tried the heron with the 200mm, which is in the shoulder bag I always carry myself. The bag also holds a gadget called a tele-extender, which makes the 200 equal to 400, but two stops slower. By the time Harum got to me, I'd tried that, too. But the bird was badly placed in reference to the camera. From where I was, he melted into the mud flats instead of being outlined against the water.

After I had the 500, which is a high-speed lens, I started edging closer to the heron and also moving to my left to put the sun against me and get some glitter on the mud, if not against the sea. It was one hell of a mess. The mud got deeper and deeper, and I was more and more determined to get an absolute full page or a double truck out of the situation. I had a fairyland of carved coral about fifty yards away: brown, like the mud, but formed into crazy shapes—shapes that still showed splashes of the water left on the coral at high tide.

I was up to my knees in mud when I finally stepped into a really deep hole. My feet couldn't go any farther, and since I was indomitably pressing forward, I went flat on my Nikon (around my neck) into the mud. The short zoom was on then and sucked up quite a load of salty mud. It is now out of combat for the rest of this assignment.

Overleaf:
One of Udjong
Kulon's largest birds,
a reef heron, also
lands at Tjisimpang.

Sinaga leads the men
ashore across the mud
flats at Tjisimpang.

The reef heron slowly searches the shallow edge of the sea for small fish.

The camera was still okay. I had the 200mm lens in one hand, the 500 in the other, held above the mud. Meanwhile my lovely bird had not gone away. He was working along the shore; with his outstretched neck—a fierce plunge—and with a silvery fish in his long beak, this heron looked and behaved as if he were straight out of Crockett Cove in Vinalhaven.

Harum came and took the two lenses, and I pulled myself up. I had to put my hands down into the mud and grab my boot tops or I'd have left the boots behind. The suction was that fierce.

A happy ending—I hope. For I reached the point I wanted, and did the heron with the rocks and without, vertical and horizontal, small and large. I was rather unsteady, and my glasses were misted over with salt spray, as were the lenses, which I kept wiping; so at the end just for security, I tried for some tripod pictures from an outcropping of coral.

Some of this has to be okay technically. Artistically it was a triumph. Especially a Polaroid snap I had Sinaga make of me with mud up to my thighs.

Monday, September 4, 3 P.M.

It's Labor Day back home. I'm sure Joan is giving a big party on Crockett Cove. She missed July Fourth, and this is the only other big weekend of the summer. I hope she is having a party, and that Elin and Jill are having a wonderful time. Me, I'm thrilled because I'm back in my tower, after what was some sortie.

Yesterday at 11 A.M., when Sinaga, I, and six men had traveled about three kilometers westward on the southern coast, I began to think that it would be stupid to go to the mouth of the Tjikevsik, which is just a few kilometers from a patrol path going most of the way back to the tower, and then to return to the isthmus, cross that, and go through that incredible mud bank again to return to the *Harini* and spend ten or so hours pitching about on it on the way back to the tower. So I made a battlefield decision and sent Amir and Enang back to the warden's station at Karangrandjang, where we'd spent the night Saturday. They were to pack up the gear we left there, then recross the isthmus and get help from the *Harini*. After Amir and Enang, and their helpers, had loaded the gear on the *Harini*, they were to take the *Harini* back to headquarters. Sinaga, I, and the other four men would walk all the way west to the patrol path, about fifteen kilometers, and then across the western end to the tower.

Our group walked a little better than fifteen kilometers yesterday, most of it on sand. Luckily the sand was well packed generally. We followed the great crescent beach westward all day, under a really blazing equatorial sun.

A walk like this is very different from one along densely shaded jungle trails. Here the sun bounces off the bright sand. The beach was littered for several miles with the debris of a Norwegian freighter, the *Torshall,* from Sandefjord, which ran aground when headed for the Sunda Strait. Enormous hardwood logs were also spread out every which way; the last storm had flung them about like so many giant matchsticks, though they weighed tons apiece. Two skeleton armchairs, half a life raft from which I took the name, and thousands of gray painted boards were also strewed about the beach. So were thirty or so large pieces of Styrofoam (which I could surely use in Maine to extend my floating dock). All the *Torshall's* seamen got off alive. The only death was that of the captain.

The surf was unbelievable, and I photographed it every possible way during the day and a half we walked near it. Yesterday we passed the mouth of the Tjikevsik, where we were supposed to camp (and then retrace our steps), and pushed on to the Tjitandahon, where the water is not too salty, to make our camp. A long, very hot walk.

Before we pushed off today I photographed our campsite, at the edge of the river. The Tjitandahon is very different from anything else I've seen in Java. Palms, their fronds festooned with small-leaved bright green vines, dip into its quiet waters, decorating them and making the whole scene look just the way one imagines Java should look.

Our men carry the equipment along the beach under the blazing sun.

he author with arum after stepping to a deep mud hole hile trying to otograph the heron.

verleaf: he Tjikevsik comes om the hills on the ght to meet the sea the southern shore.

We reached the Tjibunar at 9:35 and made a sort of break-fast-lunch there. Sohib cooked some shellfish, one of which, a univalve that clings to the rocks and resembles a small abalone, I photographed first. I ate shellfish of the same kind, in close to the same place, about three weeks ago. Today I learned that this is a "ketompo" in Sundanese, the language of western Java. I don't know how many languages Indonesia has, but several of its many islands have a half dozen each.

I also photographed a baby sea turtle this morning. One of the men caught it at the edge of the surf. The turtle was as small as the souvenir turtles sold on Broadway (you used to be able to have your name painted on the shell), but it will grow up—if it's lucky enough to grow up—to weigh a quarter of a ton or more. We let it go on the first wave that caught it.

Right now my big peacock is walking by the tower window. I guess I'm going to do him again.

I was wrong. Just opening the window shade offended him, sending him into the bushes. At this point I don't care. I'm exhausted.

I did some more botanical photography on this trip. I'd been seeing a beautiful pink bud that bursts open into a big feathery flower called the "djambu" in Indonesian, and another plant, the "pulus," belonging to the genus Laportea, I was told, that's bright green and grows up into a tree. The tree has leaf scars like those on the sumac and is very poisonous. If you touch the bark or a leaf, you get a very hard-to-heal rash. I know, because I had one on my left forearm for a week after the survey. So many of these trees fringe the beach from the Tjikevsik to the Tjitandahon, and there are so many more of them west of there that I had the men wash all my gear with soap and water when we reached the Tjibunar; I was sure the tripod and cases had banged into at least one "pulus" along the trail.

I'm really too tired to write about all this. I'm going to try to take a nap, or at least I'm going to lie down. A few minutes ago I counted my exposed film: nine rolls in three rough days.

Tuesday, September 5, 7:30 A.M.

A high wind last night, but still no rain. The wind was so strong it tore loose the lashings on the palm curtains over the missing windows and knocked over a teapot. I jumped out of bed to save my 1000mm lens, which was on a Nikon mounted on a tripod near one of the windows. Luckily I'd placed the tripod well away from the curtain, and everything was okay, but I hastily removed the camera from the tripod and put the indispensable 1000 away. Then I went back to bed. A few hours later, bang went the rattrap—waking me for good. The trap was baited with part of a banana; the rest had been brazenly eaten on my table earlier. No attention had been paid to the traditional small, dry piece of Cheddar cheese with which the trap had been baited on previous nights.

I found the old trap in the tower, and when what I thought was the rat—now it looks more like a big field mouse—had eaten into a box of crackers in the storeroom, I declared war. Bananas okay; but no crackers or spaghetti or egg noodles or sugar—or anything in paper boxes. (All the boxes of food are now in the tin case I carried my film in. Rats and mice won't eat film; only the Nikons do that.)

While we were on sortie this week two men, one of whom was Kiflie, were left behind to guard the tower. Kiflie was so infected that I gave him a full three-day course of Achromycin plus multivitamins. Sunday, feeling better, he caught a fair-sized monitor lizard with a bamboo spring trap. The lizard is now glaring up at me from the ground near the tower. The men have fastened a rope around his body, just in front of his hind legs, so he can't get away. Last night he ate the bones and the

mall-leafed vines overed the palms and ees at our campsite ear the mouth of the 'jitandahon.

skin of some fish I had for dinner. The *Harini* still isn't back, but this was a fish, a "talang," I'd put in the refrigerator the day we left.

The men are also trying to trap a barking deer. I may be able to get one on Peutjang. They are there, and I am going back to the Peutjang blind. Another thing on the agenda is building a really solid blind at the big rhino wallow. I've changed my mind again about how this blind should be built. I want it in living trees.

When we left Karangrandjang Sunday morning, we found a beautiful set of fresh leopard tracks on the beach. The tracks were only about a hundred yards from our camp. I tried to photograph them going down the beach, but how can you make that look sinister?

I recalled the leopard tracks I'd seen near the Tjibunar three weeks ago. Then Sinaga told me of a leopard he had seen when he and Talbot were in the sanctuary in 1964. Talbot had gone to sleep, and Sinaga and two other members of the 1964 survey team were sitting near the fire. Suddenly a full-grown black leopard, plainly visible in the bright moonlight, had walked up to within ten yards of the fire. Sinaga said he and the other two men just sat paralyzed; and then the leopard was gone.

Black leopards aren't uncommon here. Their favorite food is pig, and Sunday morning, after I saw the tracks, I asked Sinaga if it would be possible to trap a pig and use it for leopard bait. The pig could be placed under a tree, and I'd wait nearby—with a strobe ready, since the bait would almost certainly not be approached except after dark. But the men are Moslems; they do not eat pork. And they don't know how to trap pigs. A pit might do, covered with twigs and earth. But I'll think about this later; right now, a rhino, not a leopard, is my primary target.

We may be stretching sanctuary regulations on trapping from time to time, but Sinaga is a senior warden and so far hasn't offered any objections. Of course, we don't kill any animals—just photograph them, then let them go.

Speaking of not killing anything, I was very lucky this morning. I'd just returned to the tower from the john, which is screened by palm leaves and has large trees overhead, when I felt something tickle the back of my neck. Instead of crushing it, I brushed it off—and discovered it was a stick insect, something I was really looking for and had never seen. It does look like a stick. I put it in an empty coffee can, and it is now in the refrigerator, getting cooled down so it will sit still for a picture and look natural.

September 5, 3 P.M.

The walking stick—I think you can call it that—still isn't chilled enough. A while ago I tried the ethyl chloride on a wasp that came in; the wasp died, so I'll keep trying the cooling system.

I have a big butterfly net now. Made it from an old face net —one of those things that goes over your hat and down into your shirt—I had with me. I bought it many years ago when I was doing a story, "The Green Arctic," on the Mackenzie River delta, near where the Mackenzie empties into the Arctic Ocean. The black flies around there in the spring are beyond belief.

Remembering the Mackenzie, I can't help thinking of an old character who had a potato farm there. Because there are twenty-four hours of sun in June, he did quite well in the short summer. One winter he had brought in a dozen Irish potatoes to be used for planting the next spring. To keep them from freezing, he'd worn them inside his long underwear, above his belt. Then he'd built a small hut to live in, and stored the potatoes there. But on one of his absences to his trapline (foxes, wolverines, minks, and muskrats) his squaw wife raided the hoard and ate half of the potatoes. He almost killed her when he got back. Happily he didn't, and the six potatoes that were left multiplied well enough to provide him, after a few years, with a full acre of offspring. Irish potatoes grow here in Java too, and are excellent. For dinner last night I had some boiled ones with my "talang."

3:30 P.M. The *Harini* just arrived. It seems two fishing canoes broke down near Tamandjaja, and the *Harini* had to tow them to Labuan. That's where the *Harini* comes from, so I believe this with a grain of salt. No matter.

Everyone is laughing about our rooster. We bought him from the lighthouse people, who were leaving, and to our dismay discovered that he gets up a good half-hour before dawn and really cock-a-doodle-doos. Everyone hates him. So do the other chickens, because he runs them off when rice is scattered for all of them. So I took him along on this last sortie and left him at Karangrandjang, where he was to be our last evening's dinner. When we changed the logistics, and only Amir and Enang returned to Karangrandjang, poor Amir got stuck with the task of bringing the rooster back to the *Harini,* and just now, back to the tower, where he is carrying on as usual. I almost feel that he's been granted a reprieve. But our sleep is more important than his luck. So he goes tomorrow.

Wednesday, September 6, 10 A.M.

The landing in the mud Saturday was worse than I knew. Underneath the mud was very sharp coral, and three men have nasty cuts on their feet. I've been treating them since yesterday, when I noticed Sohib tying a dirty rag around one toe with a piece of vine. This morning one of the *Harini* men came to ask me to treat a cut on his hand. I am now a doctor. Kiflie, who had the very bad infection and could hardly walk, is okay now after fourteen capsules of Achromycin in three days (Saturday, Sunday, and Monday). He also got multivitamin pills for these three days, and for Tuesday, yesterday, and today, too. One of the other men is very jealous of all this pill-giving, so I gave him a salt tablet this morning.

The final insult to my baking: this morning the chickens, minus their former lord and master—he met his end early—actually refused the biscuits I made yesterday. I give up.

Later this morning I got the stick insect out of the refrigerator. He's about the size of a praying mantis but very slender. I photographed him on some green leaves.

September 6, 7 P.M.

Sometimes things can go too far. At noon Amir and I were about to board the *Harini* to go over to Peutjang, dive on the coral reef if the wind wasn't too strong, and then go to the rusa blind. Just as our canoe reached the *Harini,* four men came out of the forest along the path that starts at the lighthouse on the Sunda Strait. They were carrying a litter, and Amir said, "Someone is sick or dead." We immediately paddled back to shore.

The men identified themselves as from the crew of sixty the government had landed last week (the crew had arrived on a big steamer from Sumatra) to build a new lighthouse. On the litter was one of the women cooks—sick, not dead. She'd been sick for several days, the men said. Could the *Harini* run her to Labuan, eleven hours away, where there was a medical assistant?

She looked rather bad but had no temperature. I could not really determine what was wrong. She was obviously very sick and seemed very weak. Amir speaks a little English and I tried without much success to learn what was wrong. Amir thought she had been "very hot" before. So I gave her some antibiotics and aspirin, enough to last until she sees the medical assistant in Labuan. Since the Schenkels are late, there is also a good chance of her seeing them in Labuan when they arrive. Then Amir and I helped the men get her aboard the *Harini.*

By the time it left it was after three o'clock. Most of the afternoon was gone. Nevertheless, Amir and I took the canoe and went over to Peutjang—just to do the coral reef.

The tide was very low, which allowed me to shoot from above water. I tried using a face mask and sneakers, but the swell from the waves threw me into the coral, some of which is very sharp and infectious. The water was murky, so I gave up trying to work in it and stayed above the surface.

The reef is one of the most varied collections of colors, shapes, textures—and one of the weirdest sights—I have ever seen in nature. More about this tomorrow.

Thursday, September 7, 7 A.M.

The small birds are in the flowering bushes in front of the tower again. I've been trying to do them, but the wind is so strong that the twigs keep going in and out of the frame, making it almost impossible to focus. I'm still looking for an outstanding picture in which a bird, fruit, and a full purple flower are all well composed in the same frame.

Many species of coral are briefly exposed by an extreme low tide off Peutjang Island.

Getting back to the coral garden of yesterday, up to then the best coral reef I'd ever seen I saw during the *Varua* voyage, in the islands near the Solomons. The Peutjang reef is both beautiful and ugly. It even has the beauty of great ugliness.

This soft coral resembles a grotesque multi-fingered glove manipulated by the sea.

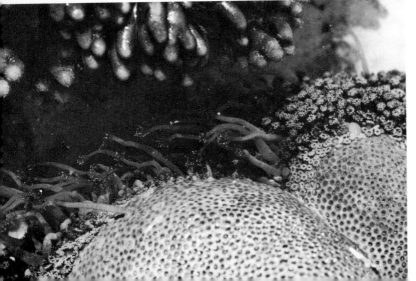

The fringe at the bottom of this large round coral is alive and constantly in motion.

Some of the corals in the Peutjang reef are very much alive. Do you call them animals? I think they are; certainly they're not plants.

Almost everyone's familiar with small pieces of coral that look like a brain; often they're brought home by sailors. I don't know where it came from, but when I was a child there was even a small coral "brain" on a table in the living room of our tenement home on New York's Seventh Street. The Peutjang coral bed has many "brains," it also has perfect mounds that look like monster basketballs cut in half; also, fans of blue, yellow, and amber, some emerging into the air at low tide. And there are some really ugly corals in the Peutjang bed. One in particular looked like a grotesque rubbery glove with forty or fifty fat fingers, each of them deformed in a slightly different way. The fingers, lying on a rock, were soft; they moved gently with the swishing sea, and you knew they were alive. The big "basketballs" have a fringe at bottom, all around, of inch-long tentacles; the tentacles, which look like a fancy hem on a skirt, wave gently in the water. I found one coral that was brilliant green;

A Tridacna *clam capable of growing to a width of three feet is enclosed by a live coral.*

another was battleship gray; and two types had bright blue tips on their spiny branches.

One thing truly fascinated me: an old friend, the tridacna, the clam that grows to mammoth size and has a wavy-edged shell. In Maine we're using half of a tridacna shell as a bird bath, but it's only about fourteen inches across; I've seen them a yard wide. Tridacnas are sometimes called man-eaters, but this is only a figure of speech. However—and this is an unlikely prospect—if you were unlucky enough to put your hand or foot into one of these giant clams (while diving, say), you would be anchored by hundreds of pounds below. The wavy slit of the live tridacna, called the mantle, is brilliant blue-green flesh; if you split a tridacna open, you'll find that this lip of flesh goes all around the inside edge of the shell.

In the Peutjang reef some of the tridacna clams had anchored themselves on small pieces of coral—only to have the coral grow around them. Four were completely enmeshed in balls of coral, with only their lips and a tiny bit of shell left uncovered. I wondered how such a clam can live. Maybe it's crushed by the coral, and dies; or maybe it stays alive, but small (for how could it grow?). I couldn't tell.

Photographed one of the coral-enmeshed clams for its beauty —the wavy lips centered in a rich beige group of "brain" convolutions. Then I did another, not so pretty, which I wanted for the record, to show that the first was not a phenomenon.

If I go to the reef again—perhaps toward the end of my stay in Udjong Kulon—I'll go fully clothed instead of in trunks and sneakers. Yesterday I carried the underwater exposure meter and the Nikonos camera, but it wasn't easy. I can't wear my glasses, which won't fit under the tight faceplate, so I must memorize the meter and camera settings. I think I have some fine coral pictures, especially those in which to get a feeling of location and space; I used the landscape of the peninsula as a backdrop.

I'd intended to do the Peutjang blind yesterday, and perhaps also today, for deer and whatever else came. But not now, with the *Harini* away on its mercy mission to Labuan. I will not attempt another crossing in a dugout canoe.

When we came back from the island yesterday afternoon, the canoe was headed directly into the wind—a wind stiff enough to put whitecaps on the waves. It took us about twenty-five minutes to do what I estimate is a quarter of a mile, and I had to bail the canoe several times to keep the water in the bottom from reaching our equipment platform. There's not much point in making the hazardous crossing again today. Better to stay here and wait for the *Badak*, which is due back later, or the *Harini*, due tomorrow, to take me on my next trip to the island.

mal is and how prettily he or she fits into the compositions of palms and a stark white dead tree.

I'll stay at the coast, get up before dawn, about 5 A.M., and be in the blind by first light, at 6:30. Then back to the tent around noon, when the rhinos supposedly go to sleep.

I'm confident I'll get a rhino—if only it rains enough to get some mud in the wallow. I even had a complete roof put on the blind so the birds won't give it away. I'll have either Harum or Enang with me, and either of them can, I'm told, actually smell a rhino.

The Schenkels did not agree that the rhino sleeps in the afternoon. So the blind has been made large enough to sleep in. I may have to spend several days in this tree house, not even climbing down to stretch my legs.

This morning, when we were about halfway from the tower to the campsite, I found a strangler fig in fruit. Three great hornbills, a squirrel, and several monkeys left with our arrival. I wasn't looking for these animals, but I'm going to look now.

The log at the right of the wallow was photographed from the same position with a 1000mm mirror lens.

We checked every other strangler fig we could find on the way. But only the one tree was in fruit. So tomorrow I'm building—or rather, having built—a new blind. It is to be on a platform about twenty feet up the side of several trees with a fair view of the branches of the fruiting fig, and I expect to start working it the day after tomorrow, while there's still ripe fruit.

I'm really busy now, but only during the twelve daylight hours. The evenings bother me. Dinner is over at about 6:30, or it would be too dark to manage to cook and all. I try to stay up by reading or fiddling with the radio. I should have spent the $50 in Djakarta to buy a special three-band shortwave set. You need one out here. I do have one shortwave band, but it's not very powerful. The wind can almost change the station. Also, it's nearly impossible to tune accurately; it pulls in too much static.

I've been sweating out the arrival of the Schenkels on the *Badak*. They were due yesterday evening. They left on the 31st, early in the morning, and still aren't back. They are bringing my mail and cables, and since Take 1, the first batch of film I did, went out with Talbot on August 18, there should be some reaction to it from New York. I'm still thinking of going to Djakarta myself on the 19th. If I do, I may try to telephone New York. I'm really getting very restless—need to know what results on the pictures so far, and to have some encouragement.

Being here is almost like being in solitary confinement. Sinaga withdraws so quickly that I can't really cope with it. This is, I'm told, typically Indonesian.

Harum was point man this morning—in the lead so he could spot game well before I came up to it. He was going a little too slowly. So, very politely, and very quietly, I asked Sinaga to move him along. Sinaga obliged, and so did Harum. Then, just a few minutes later, Harum didn't wait for us when we stopped to look at something. This was bad because he had some of the equipment and also because any game would be gone by the time we came up. I asked Sinaga please to tell Harum not to go too far ahead. At this, Sinaga assumed a hurt expression; his head drooped—and I gave up.

Sinaga has it hard with me too. But I refrain now from any possible criticism. Wednesday, when he was on his way to the rhino wallow, Sinaga encountered the group carrying the sick woman toward our camp. Instead of coming back to interpret —he knows Amir speaks a little, inadequate English—he just let the group go on, for Amir and me to cope with as best we could. I didn't say anything about this—no point in it.

It's after five now, and time to start thinking about dinner. Lunch was a picnic: two slices of pumpernickel and half a can of tomato herring. The others ate the rest of the can of herring along with their rice, beans, fried peanuts, and salted fish.

Waiting now for the *Harini* to return. Anxiously, since I can't really go anywhere without it.

September 8, 6:30 P.M.

Dinner on the light side, in spite of the meager lunch. If you eat too much, it's hard to fall asleep.

I'm still eating the rooster which crowed too early and too

often. Had rooster soup tonight, with the back, liver, and heart; added some canned lima beans and a boiled potato to the soup, making it more filling. After that, two baked plantains—small ones, the two together about as big as a typical banana—with as much honey as I could get on one fork dip. It's rather a wide fork, and honey sticks to it, and this is enough and also sporting. I'm using S & W California Sage Honey, which is delicious; I've almost finished the first of two jars. Have about one tablespoon of peanut butter left in my first jar of four. Still have to finish my first can of Australian apricot jam. My next jam will be strawberry, not the wild strawberry my Vinalhaven neighbors gave me—I'm still saving that—but a two-pound can of Gant's (from South Africa) that I bought in Bukavu in the Congo. Threw it in with my camping gear when I came back from there earlier this year, and on impulse, in with the gear I was taking here. It's the most traveled and expensive can of jam in the world. It ends here.

No *Harini,* no *Badak* today. Sad. Mail late now. Looked for so eagerly.

Saturday, September 9

It's about 5 P.M., and I'm mad at everybody—especially myself and Pat Hunt. The *Badak* and *Harini* both arrived last night. Both the Schenkels were sick with dysentery; hence the delay.

The mail and cables came this morning. By some miracle, there was even a response to Take 2, which didn't leave here until the 31st; it got to New York, was processed, was looked at, and on the 5th a cable about it was sent to Djakarta. Fantastic! Why am I mad? Pat Hunt's only comments were, "Worried about peacock and dragon lizard shots in flat light in plain setting giving too ordinary look to pictures. Pictures do not suggest Indonesian setting." There was also a cable sent August 31 in response to Take 1, delivered by Talbot August 25: "Take 1 looks good"; also, "completely covered exposure- and picture-wise." Take 2 had forty-two rolls of blood-earned film—and I get asked for Indonesian atmosphere. Do they expect Balinese dancers in the background?

My back still hurts from that underwater strain, and now I have the trots too. Even some of the men have them. This morning I ran a check on our water supply and discovered that the men were bathing fifty feet downstream from where the water is drawn. I'm sure Talbot ordered otherwise. Another thing: the men have been utilizing the river as a toilet. They've been doing it fairly far downstream, but not far enough to suit me. Since the bathing place is well established, I designated another place to get water upstream; I also ordered a stop to all bathroom activities except at the mouth of the river, near the beach.

All my water, even for cooking, is preboiled, but washing of dishes and glasses and utensils is all in water straight from the river. I may have stopped this outbreak of dysentery. I hope so. I have Lomotil, an excellent medicine for this.

There are an awful lot of problems for one man to cope with. And now Sinaga is sick again. Last night he told me he had to go home. I must allow him.

On Peutjang there is a young trainee who graduated from forestry school, then came to work with Dr. Schenkel for experience. He speaks English and will come over to the mainland today so Sinaga can start training him in his duties. His name is Sutrisno.

Sinaga is leaving Wednesday, on the *Harini.* I intend to go to Labuan on the *Badak* on the 18th—the Schenkels decided to send it out then instead of on the 19th—and to have a car from Djakarta waiting to pick me up. Sinaga will ask Amir Daud to arrange the car. I'll spend the 19th in Djakarta getting my visa renewed, possibly visiting the zoo, and checking some of my camera equipment and will leave there at 4 A.M. in order to catch the *Badak* when it gets the high tide out of Labuan at 8 A.M. on the 20th. The channel at Labuan hasn't been dredged since Indonesian independence and is almost completely blocked with sand except at high tide.

Monday, September 11, 3:20 P.M.

In the new blind about twenty feet above the ground near the strangler fig that's in fruit. Have been here most of the day. Originally planned to come here yesterday, but yesterday I was trying to rest my back, which is better today.

So far I've seen three types of hornbill: the rhinoceros hornbill, *Buceros rhinoceros,* a huge one I never saw before which has a bright orange beak and an extra upper beak that's curved backward like a scimitar; the wreathed hornbill, *Rhyticeros undulatus,* a large yellow-beaked one with brown feathers on the back of his head and a blue bag on his neck; and a smaller one with a black and white breast and black and white tail called the pied hornbill, *Anthracoceros malabaricus.* I've also seen black crows, which seem to be everywhere, some birds which look like wood pigeons with greenish wings, and many smaller birds, including a barbet. A yellow-tailed squirrel has been busy on the branches, and a smaller, lazy black one has been eating fruit on the ground. All wonderful to see, but I'm too low and have to look up at the birds, and through a screen of foliage. Once in a while a bird or squirrel breaks out of the mass and into the clear; you have to be ready then.

This morning a banteng family decided to graze and rest nearby. I left the blind and did the bantengs with two crows,

*interior of a tree
se built near a
ngler fig tree in
 with the author
ling a Nikon F
era with a 500mm
·or lens.*

A wreathed hornbill eating a fig.

Two pied hornbills in the same tree.

The rhinoceros hornbill's beak is orange.

which pecked away at their backs—eating insects. In Africa a bird called the oxpecker dines the same way. Last year, in Kenya, I photographed two of these red-billed birds (with Mount Kilimanjaro as a background). They worked so hard on a rhinoceros that they actually went through his hide and drew blood. Another African bird cleans crocodiles' teeth of tidbits while the crocs snooze with their mouths open. I saw this done at the bottom of Murchison Falls.

Sohib caught a snake early this morning—green with some indistinct stripes, about twenty inches long, and very slender. He was very aggressive. We looped the bottom of his tail, tied a nylon string on the loop, and attached the string to a small stake driven into the ground. We then threw a lot of tan and brown leaves around for photographic contrast.

The snake, a very nice character, kept climbing up on a twig to strike at me. Even though he was tied, I always jumped back. Especially since I was trying to do close-ups at four to six inches from his head. I didn't know if he was poisonous or not, but I always presume unidentified snakes are. We let him go.

A yellow-tailed squirrel climbs the fig tree to feed on the ripe fruit.

Saw the Schenkels later this morning (they came over to our beach before setting out for the Tjibunar), and they told me they'd just killed two small snakes near their camp. They be-

lieved them to be coral snakes—corals of a very deadly variety. I carry a snakebite kit every time I leave camp. Have one here in the blind with me, for it's a forty-five minute walk through the woods to get back to the tower from here. From the description I gave the Schenkels, they identified Sohib's catch as a whip snake, and poisonous.

It is now 3:40, and things have slowed down considerably. I'm thinking of having Sinaga and the crew come here tomorrow morning and put up another platform, fifteen feet higher than this one. Perhaps something as simple as a hidden seat at the top of another ladder would serve to get me past the obstructing foliage. Need to do this while the strangler still has ripe fruit.

Strange that none of the other stranglers are in fruit. But if one is, the others shouldn't be far behind.

Most of the men are on Peutjang today, building a new rusa blind. The deer are farther north on the island now, so a new blind may give me better luck on close-ups of these beauties. The fruit bats that sometimes live on the northwest corner of the island still aren't back. They are obviously in another area, with ripe fruit. No one seems to know where this is. I am presuming they will come back.

Tuesday, September 12, 11 A.M.

Just woke up Harum and Enang. We're at the new Peutjang blind, away from any path. We practically had to step over a pig family to get in. There are holes in the sides of the blind, a foot or so from the floor; I had them cut so that Harum and Enang could watch for deer while sitting down. This was a mistake, because while I was reading over what I'd written in the diary during the past few days, they fell asleep. They can see twice as far and twice as quickly. But only when their eyes are open.

I'm losing Harum when the *Badak* leaves on the 18th. He has to take care of his farm. I'm also losing two of the porters. I have a replacement for Harum: Anda, an excellent tracker from the Forestry Department who led one of the survey teams last month. Anda is alert-looking, moves quickly, and is very poised. Because he has been with Professor Schenkel he is accustomed to foreigners and eager to please. Harum has heard that he has a new baby girl. He's naming her Elioti. Very flattering.

This morning I had some good luck—for a change. When we took off for Peutjang I decided to have the *Harini* go around the northwest corner of the island, where the fruit bats sometimes hang out. Literally, because they hang upside down, suspended by their claws from the branches.

160

I waited on the *Harini,* which was anchored about a hundred yards from the shore, and sent Harum to the shore to scare bats into the air. Soon the sky was almost black with them. We tried using the walkie-talkies as previously planned, but one of the two sets was not working well, too much humidity probably. I had three cameras ready with 55, 200, and 300mm lenses; one camera held Kodachrome, the other two, high-speed Ektachrome. Did some shots showing the shore and the trees and the sky, and others (with the 300mm) just showing the bats.

I'll hit them again this afternoon, after they've had a chance to settle down a bit. (We watched them return to the trees before we left for the blind.) Around 3 or 4 P.M. I should have a good sidelight on them.

While we were on the way to the blind, Harum ran a line behind the *Harini* and had a strike from so large a fish that the line broke. I must try to get a heavier line in Djakarta.

Just glanced over at Enang, sitting with eight strips of plaster I put over infected tick bites on his legs last night. Sinaga, who's leaving tomorrow, has a swollen arm, we think from a scorpion bite. It has responded somewhat to antihistamine pills; cortisone ointment did nothing for it. My back is almost completely well. This sounds like a medical report. Sinaga also has two infected tick spots, which I'm treating with antibiotic salve. I'm treating another man, who looks generally sick, with multivitamins.

Sinaga, the new man, Sutrisno, and all the others except Harum and Enang, who are here with me, left for the rusa blind around 7 this morning. They're building a new platform, which will be about fifteen feet higher than and reached by a ladder from the first one. Then, above the new platform, to be reached by another ladder, they're building a seat—a sort of a crow's nest, which will really get me up above the foliage that was getting in my way yesterday. I go back tomorrow, while the fruit lasts.

September 12, 12:15 P.M.

We've just had lunch in the Peutjang rusa blind; some boiled rice, a can of tomato herring, some onion, and two cucumbers, which Harum, Enang, and I shared.

Nothing has shown up yet. And the men are awake. It's very humid today, but no rain. A while back the Schenkels showed me a tin hurricane lamp that had been brought to the peninsula three months ago; the top was rusted off. My tripods, knife blades, etc., have to be touched with an oily rag every few days; otherwise they'd rust away. I can imagine what it's like in the rainy season. Even now the wind blows almost all the time. It's noisy, but makes the temperature bearable. I didn't bring a

thermometer (except medical), so I don't know the range. I do know you sometimes need to cover yourself at night.

12:35 P.M. Still nothing here. But something has to come. Harum and Enang still alert.

The trees around the rusa blind are magnificent—huge and tall, with widely buttressed bases. Heavy vines twist around them, snaking their way upward. The ground is littered with leaves, mostly brown but occasionally pink or even mauve. Shafts of sunlight accent the vine-clad tree trunks, falling now here, now there as the leaf cloud above sways in the wind. Birds fly by, not seen, but heard. The weirdest noise of all: two tree trunks touching, grinding at each other, like an old house creaking.

12:50. A great big beautiful male rusa. He walked right up to the blind, but from a side where, because of the wind, no tripod was set. I took a chance with the 300mm, 1/125 at F4.5,

Rusa stags claim a particular place in the forest as their territory and stop other males from encroaching.

hand held; some of the shots just have to be okay. He didn't scare off; finally just walked behind a dense group of trees—not to show again.

Wait . . . now he's moving.

No luck. He moved far enough around to get our scent. Won't see him again today.

I have only half of him in most of the shots because I used the 300, which was in my hands when he arrived. If I'd paused to change cameras, I probably would have lost him. I would have preferred some more atmosphere, but you can't hold several telephotos without cutting your neck in two.

Will stay in the blind until about 2:30. Then off to try for the fruit bats again.

Wednesday, September 13, 11 A.M.

The *Harini* left at dawn this morning for Labuan, taking Sinaga, Harum, Kadir, and Kiflie along. Mr. Djuhari, the chief game warden of Udjong Kulon who had been staying with the Schenkels, also hitched a ride. I was truly sorry to see them go. Sinaga has a cable to give Daud to send to New York asking Pat Hunt for a specific list of subjects still not covered adequately. I also need to know when this essay goes to press. There will be no point in continuing to take pictures that cannot make this issue.

I am back at the strangler fig blinds. I've never done any high-wire acrobatics, or been a steeplejack, but I feel like a combination acrobat-steeplejack now, for I've just been up to the third, or top, platform. It's about the same size as the platform a high-wire artist steps out from. It's some fifty feet from the forest floor. And there is no net.

I cannot describe adequately what the three crazy platforms look like up in the air. Won't even try.

The variety of birds is large. The spectacular ones are the hornbills. Have already seen the same three types I saw here Monday—the huge orange-billed one, the big one with the bluish goiter-like appendage on its throat, and the small one with the black and white breast and tail. Noticed this morning that the small one, which is yellow billed, has white marks on its wings. Another bird, one of the barbets, is about the size of a robin; it is predominantly green, two shades of green, has a black, aggressive beak, a yellow cap, and red spots on its face. It loves figs.

Just watched the huge hornbill pick up a fig with his scimitar-like bill. He held it for a moment, then threw back his head and let the pill—I mean fruit—slide down his throat.

Many long-tailed squirrels know about the strangler too. They sit on its limbs, holding on with their hind feet; the body droops forward, and the tail, on the other side of the limb, gives

165

balance. Each fruit is eaten daintily. Sometimes one of the squirrels will hang by its tail to pick a particularly succulent fruit below—and will even eat while thus suspended.

September 13, 12:30 P.M.

Had lunch on deck two, which is fairly stable; then back up to the crow's nest again.

I've discovered that hornbills can be nasty. One drives the others away from the branch he is feeding on. This is one of the orange-double-bill types. The type with the bluish goiter is a less frequent visitor; none has been around since this morning. All the birds are almost continually hopping about. I keep hoping that they'll reach a fairly clear space, where I can get an entire bird. Sometimes they do.

I'm very happy with most of the pictures I'm getting. Before, the birds were just fast-moving objects in the sky. Now I can count their features, or see one whose lower bill is slightly broken on the right side.

Yesterday afternoon I had the sky full of fruit bats again. Now I need a colorful butterfly or two and I'll have taken care of the air.

September 13, 3 P.M.

Had to pack up. Not seasick; but too much wind for photography. Will come back tomorrow at noon, since the light is better after the morning.

Thursday, September 14, 7:45 A.M.

Very cloudy this morning, but no rain.

Swaying around in the wind yesterday made me forget our first crocodile, which was here sometime Tuesday night or perhaps just before dawn yesterday morning. As soon as I got up yesterday one of the men called me to see the fresh track.

The croc was at least six or eight feet long, and its body was almost as thick as mine. It came from the sea, scraped its way across the narrow beach of sand, and entered the Tjidaon, from which we get our water. The weight of its body made a smooth, continuous depression in the sand, and the distance apart of the deep toe marks indicated the croc's size.

By coincidence the *Harini* men caught a small shark (about three feet long) in their net early yesterday morning. It's just as well that the sea in front of our beach is so shallow that, even at high tide, it isn't worth swimming in. It's very different on Peutjang. There the shore drops off into deep water almost as soon as you leave the beach, but the beach is fringed with lots of sharp coral. You can't win here.

On the way back to the tower yesterday afternoon I found

trangler fig tree
it, which at-
d the birds, is on
ft of the three
ouses from
we worked.

one of the long-tailed squirrels on the ground. He looked alive but was stone dead. Somehow he must have fallen and broken his neck. I took the opportunity to study his very nicely marked coat and his extra-long front incisors. Anda put him on a tree trunk using the toenails for support.

There's a lot of the fruit the barking deer like between the tower and my strangler fig. The trail is littered with regurgitated pits.

Last year, on the Serengeti plains, I watched the wild dogs go out in packs from their lairs, which are holes in the ground large enough so that the dogs appear and disappear like characters in a comic opera. The young stay home, where they're guarded by the wounded (I saw two limpers) and by members of the family too old to run down an antelope. The pack runs its prey down, tearing at it all the time, for these animals don't have killing jaws, like the hyena, or weight and strength, like

The author forgot about swimming when he found this smooth crocodile slide leading into the Tjidaon.

Walking stick

Overleaf Egrets

168

Mouse deer

Foliage along the
Tjitandahon River

*Chestnut-headed
bee-eater*

Stork-billed kingfisher

Tepus blossom

Sempur blossom
and fruit

Pandanus fru

such predatory cats as lions, leopards, and cheetahs. They are said to plan their attacks with the individual pack members taking turns putting on bursts of speed. They eat their prey not only after it has fallen but also while it is being torn down. When they come home, some of them regurgitate the kill they have just eaten for those that stayed behind. The puppies fight over it. There are some related (*Cuon javanicus*), but rarely seen, animals in Udjong Kulon; like their African cousins, they have rounded ears.

The ABC group I was with in Africa last year rode in a Land Rover from which the entire top had been removed (so that a camera could make a full 360-degree turn). Once, when we were parked near a wild dog lair, two of the largest males started walking toward us—and kept getting closer . . . and closer, until when they were just fifteen feet away, I took my long hunting knife out of its sheath and held it in front of me. Finally, at about ten feet, they stopped.

Robert Ardrey was with us the next day, watching the same pack. He said that these animals' behavior was similar to that of primitive human beings. But not being strong enough to kill bare-handed, so to speak, primitive man used a bone or a stick to help him kill.

The baboons in Africa have very strong jaws, and they like meat. I saw one large baboon carry off a baby Thomson's gazelle, and begin to munch it. After he'd put a comfortable distance between us. The fact that apes are carnivorous as well as vegetarian lends credence to the theory that the most advanced ones learned to hunt with a bone or stick, and then developed to early man. I am afraid I've oversimplified this. One should read Louis Leakey, who found man's earliest remains in the Olduvai Gorge, about this, and one should certainly read Ardrey in *African Genesis*.

Leaving the tower now, to try to photograph a half-grown mouse deer in a special camouflaged corral built for him outside.

9:45 A.M. Got the mouse deer to take some milk (made from our supply of dry crystals), so he was rather frisky. He kept trying to find holes in the fence—which there aren't. He also hid under the foliage I introduced to give the corral a natural look.

West Coast
sunset

He has huge eyes and the tiniest split hoofs. He is a precious animal, small enough to fit into a basketball sneaker. The full-grown mouse deer is about the size of an African dik-dik, maybe even smaller.

Overleaf:
A captured male
mouse deer, too young
to have antlers, is
smaller than a
domestic cat.

September 14, 2 P.M.

Just back from the strangler fig where I went after an early

lunch. Yesterday the tree was like a beehive. An anthill. Action everywhere.

Today not a bird. It doesn't seem possible, but there isn't any fruit left on tree. I climbed up to the third platform, where I am only twenty feet from some of the fig branches. Yesterday they were loaded with fruit. This afternoon, empty—stripped clean by eaters and wind.

If I hadn't shot four rolls of color film yesterday, I don't know what I'd have done. Building those platforms involved a lot of effort—and danger—for the men. I don't know how I'd have justified myself for causing it. In photography you shoot when you can, not tomorrow.

The ladder to the top platform was a touch shaky today; I suppose the rattan vine holding it together has some elasticity. The worst ladder I ever climbed—even worse than that at the Sunda Strait lighthouse—was a single-rung hand-over-hand one to the top of the Streets of Paris building at the 1939 New York World's Fair. Since the ladder was about a hundred feet straight up, I was quite mad to attempt it—for a picture that didn't even get published. I was at the fair doing pictures of Gypsy Rose Lee, for *Life*. When I posed her against the building, Mike Todd, who was running the show, came out and said, "Put that on the cover and I'll buy you a suit of clothes." I was wearing tweed jackets in those days. Gypsy asked me to stay after the show and buy her a drink. I did, and began a friendship that's going still, and appreciated by both of us.

All this is being written back at my old stand: the first blind, center field in front of the tower. A massive black banteng bull is walking through the grazing ground as if he owns it. I guess he does. Not even a leopard would tackle him.

On the other edge of the field is the family, with a young one. I keep hoping the bantengs will get together for a family portrait. If they do, I think I'll feel like a winner of the daily double at a race track. You have to pick two winning horses in a row, and the odds are against—very much against—your doing it.

2:50 P.M. The bantengs just got together. I made some pictures, but the bantengs were—still are—lying down, chewing their cud. They look like so many plain ordinary cows.

Now the bull is snoozing after sniffing one of the ladies quite intimately. They and the baby have all walked off, leaving him alone. One of the cows must be in season, or almost, bringing our boy. Otherwise he wouldn't get caught dead with the women. In this respect he's very much like the African elephant, only arriving to do his duty.

I learned quite a bit about elephant behavior in Tanzania last year. One particularly interesting thing was told me by Ian Douglas Hamilton, a young Oxford ecologist, who said that all the acacia trees I saw in Lake Manyara Park had germinated from seeds that had been eaten, then excreted, by elephants. The seeds are eaten along with the pods, and when he defecates, the elephant plants them. Any seed that has not been eaten and excreted by an elephant won't germinate. But by pushing down the young trees to eat the leaves, the elephants destroy most of what they've planted.

The "sempur" tree outside this blind is getting heavier and heavier with fruit, and I'm still very hopeful that I'll be able to get the monkeys eating it. I did see several monkeys eating "sempur" flowers, and one monkey holding a green fruit. But that was a long time ago. Three weeks. I've been in Udjong Kulon only five, yet it seems that I've lived here most of my life.

4:05. Just got the two peahens—or are they young cocks?—with the group of banteng cows which returned a minute ago. Our hero, the bull, is still prone, in splendid isolation about a hundred yards to the right of the cows.

I suppose that, once, sometime, I may get them all, with crows flying from their backs, a great sky, and so on. This waiting is what is sometimes so killing about photography. If I was here as a painter instead of as a photographer, I could make notes and sketches and put everything here together in a splendid composition. But no one wants that kind of painting today; it's considered antediluvian.

When I came out to the blind, I didn't forget my pen and pad. But I don't have my . . . whatever you call what you give a baby to stop its fussing. In my case this is a plastic flask with about one ounce of whiskey to ten of water. It's hardly stronger than a soft drink, but it tastes better and keeps me quiet. I am tired.

Shot roll after roll on the tiny mouse deer this morning. He almost never held still, and the strain of focusing was enormous. Two hours of it. What worked best was setting the lens at four feet and moving back and forth with the animal, shooting when sharp. While doing this I was holding a small leafy twig in my left hand so I could dangle leaves in front of the lens to produce big out-of-focus green areas that should make the photographs look like lucky grab shots (and also give them depth and visual variety). The left hand moves in and out and up and down. The head cranes forward, then back; higher, then lower; and the dear deer buzzes around like a bee. This deer has big soulful eyes, but only when his head is up where you can see them. He also has a little white-fringed tail, and when he licks himself, shows a very long tongue.

4:20. The banteng bull is still lying there. A stork-billed bright blue kingfisher is in the foreground now, but not close enough. And there's a group of pigs—too far to the right. Otherwise everything's great.

4:30. He got up and is just standing there, sniffing. The wind is across both of us, but he must be getting a little of me, and he doesn't like it. Big, almost arrogant. White stockings on all four legs. A round white patch on his hindquarters—about the size and shape of a chamois patch on riding pants. His horns are heavy across his forehead; nothing like the African buffalo's boss, but still a solid structure from horn to horn.

He's still looking for me, and I have no intention of waving either a cape or a Nikon at him. By a coincidence I read a Hemingway bullfighter story, "The Undefeated," last night, in a collection called *Men Without Women*.

The light is going fast, but not our friend. Rooted to the spot.

No, he's moving off now. Now I can leave the blind without spooking him. They'll come again another day. I hope.

Friday, September 15, 8 A.M.

I remember tomato herring. Some people remember Mama or when they were young, but I remember tomato herring. I am in the center-field blind again, trying morning light for a change. Perhaps I can get a close-up of the big peacock with back lighting for a dramatic effect. The memories of tomato herring came up earlier this morning, as I packed my lunch bag for the Peutjang blind. I want another chance at a male rusa with full antlers this afternoon.

Tomato herring, if I had to choose the important food in my life, is it. And memories of it go back to my childhood and then jump twenty years, to stay with me, it seems, for the rest of my life. I ate can after can of it on my drive from Cape Town to Cairo in 1947. By the empty flat oval tins (labeled Pilchards in Tomato Sauce by the British packers) my trail can be traced along the east side of Africa (what Rhodes hoped would one day be all British Empire) from one end of the continent to the other. Not that I throw empty cans about. I don't; I bury them. But they might easily be found by some future archaeologist tracing migration routes.

This food is perfect for tough safaris; one can fits nicely flat in your jacket pocket or haversack and makes a good meal. There are three or four herrings in lots of tasty sauce. So it is a moist meal, and it is filling; if you have a small raw onion to chop on top of it—and I usually do—that is really good.

Here in Udjong Kulon I'm using herrings in tomato sauce from California. Sometimes they're called sardines. Actually sardines are small herrings.

There are herring fishermen on our island, Vinalhaven, in Maine, and they net these fish every year. This July I was given some freshly caught and tried marinating them. I used olive oil, wine vinegar, lemon juice, sugar, salt, pepper, fresh tarragon, and a couple of bay leaves, placed a layer of herring, then a layer of sliced red onion, then one of herring, and so on, in a quart jar. It was fabulous. Fresh herrings are also very good fried.

Herring was one of our staple foods when I was a boy on New York's Lower East Side. We always bought the salt herring, either matjes or schmaltz, put up in big barrels. The herrings would come glistening and dripping out of the murky brine and were carried home from the store in a piece of newspaper. Some were too salty and had to be soaked. Some were washed off, peeled, and served with a dressing of salad oil, vinegar diluted with some water, and a little sugar. Sliced onions and boiled potatoes completed the dish. This was when my father was working, and we could afford it. I can remember meals of only boiled potatoes flavored with the brine from some pickles my mother had put up in an earthenware crock.

My mother made a dish I really liked: herring and onions fried in salad oil. She also made chopped herring. I don't think I can remember pickled herring except store bought.

When things were rough we still had tomato herring, for in our neighborhood people were poor enough to buy a single tomato herring from a can the grocer opened each day. My mother would send us to the store to buy one or two as needed. Since herring is a food I associate with the days when I didn't have much, I might be expected to despise it. But I don't. I loved the food my mother served. I grew up loving it.

Later, things got really bad, and my mother had the good idea of taking in boarders. We called them boarders, though they came only for the evening meal. Because of their financial contribution we children—there were four of us, Belle, Edward, myself, and George—also had things like chicken and pot roast and rich soups to eat.

My mother died a few years ago, at eighty-seven, and even in her last year she made lunch for me every Saturday I was in New York. I never missed one of these lunches. They were the great enjoyment of her later years, and my pleasure too. Stuffed fish, rolled cabbage, chicken fricassee, chicken soup, and roast chicken, chopped chicken livers, borscht, schav, herring and potatoes, potato pancakes, blini—I had them all. I could hardly walk away from the table. At one of these lunches my mother told me what to her was a sad story. It seems that we children ate with the boarders, and once I had the temerity to reach out to take a favorite morsel of food from the platter on the table. A boarder stopped me by hitting my hand with the flat of his knife. My mother never forgot it, nor did she ever forgive that boarder.

It's now close to nine o'clock. Anda is in the blind with me, watching from holes cut near the bottom on three sides. So far nothing has come; one hornbill flew over, and that's all.

Almost all the activity in the grazing ground has been afternoon, but I saw the big peacock out here at 6:30 this morning.

The Schenkels are coming to dinner tonight, and last night we butchered the small goat I bought in Tamanjaja when I first came here. I avoided watching it, but unfortunately I could hear.

I'm leaving for Djakarta on Monday, the 18th, will have my visa extended, read my mail, and hopefully, have some answers to the cables I sent out with Sinaga on the 13th. I'll return here the 22nd.

I hope I'll then know where this story stands and whether *Life* will or will not wait for a possible rhino picture. The issue is at the end of the year, but some color must be engraved now. I know I've made some beautiful pictures here. But how many, and how they're appreciated, I don't know. This is not obvious material like that in Africa, and it is a very important story to me because it's one of my first major assignments for *Life* in a long time. I've been so busy with other projects that I and the right story just didn't coincide; also, out of sight, out of mind. Since I don't make my entire livelihood out of *Life* any more, I must do other work. There's also not enough to do for *Life,* for the magazine has changed from a straight picture magazine to one with a combination of pictures and text. It amazes me that the magazine can be kept fresh after more than thirty years of publishing.

I'm rambling on a good deal this morning. This is my most energetic time, and I cannot sit still. I need work.

We'll leave soon for Peutjang. Since the *Harini* is gone, we'll paddle across in the canoe—with the wind, which will make it easy. Then we'll hitch a ride on the *Badak* when the Schenkels come across for an early dinner. I must remember to hide my last can of *hopjes,* the Dutch coffee-flavored hard candy. Mrs. Schenkel is crazy about them and ate about half of the other tin I had. I still have some sour-lemon drops I bought at one of the airports where we stopped en route. Can't remember which airport—they all blend together now. I'll offer the lemon drops tonight.

September 15, 2:15 P.M.

I'm in the Peutjang blind, waiting for a male rusa. This is the second rusa blind, built Monday. Have been here for two hours now. Know I won't succeed because we—Anda, Suleman, and I—passed a rusa stag on our way to the blind. I can't tell one rusa from another, especially at a hundred yards, but so far when we see a stag while walking, no stag comes up to us later.

183

Will try for another forty-five minutes though, until three.

Got nothing in the tower grazing-ground blind this morning, and it looks like a no-hit, no-run shutout today. I'd like to have a few more good pictures to send in when I get to Djakarta on the 19th. I do have the birds and the young mouse deer. There are some big strangler figs on the way to this blind, and I looked for signs of fruit, but none so far. One of the stranglers started up in the crown of a tree at least a hundred feet high, and its roots have embraced the trunk all the way down.

Dr. Schenkel is sick again, his stomach. I asked Mrs. Schenkel, whom I saw on the way to the blind, if she wanted a consultant. She laughed and said one might be helpful; the patient didn't have too much confidence. So I prescribed Lomotil, a new drug for diarrhea and dysentery; she agreed, and we'll give him some tonight.

Even with the wind, the canoe trip across the channel was very choppy. But Suleman and Anda are both excellent water men. The *Badak* will take us back.

I'm sitting here thinking about my film. With luck, Take 3 should be in New York tomorrow, and I may hear results on the 19th. I hope Daud sends my mail to Labuan on that car that's to pick me up on the 18th.

Saturday, September 16, 3 P.M.

I'm in one of two new blinds built near the tower this morning. This one is in far left field, at the very end of the grazing ground, which borders here on the banks of the Tjidjung Kulon. The Tjidjung Kulon is wide, a pretty river but too salty for daily use. I had the blind made where it turns, so I can look either upstream or down. At high tide, in about an hour, some of the men are going to drag our canoe over the sandbank into the river so I can paddle up it very quietly early tomorrow and see what I can get. Hopefully, I'll get some birds. I particularly want kingfishers, and very particularly, a fine white egret. The egret, which rose too quickly for me to photograph when I was reconnoitering to find new places to build blinds, is the reason I decided to have this one built.

The second new blind is halfway between here and the first, center-field blind built in the tower area. The bantengs and peacocks and pigs have been coming into the area from the east, and I want to be closer to them. I especially want to be closer to the big banteng bull—while he's still being intrigued by the female group.

A tiny sandpiper almost flew into the blind just now. Gave his unusual "whit, whit." Then flew off.

I can afford to have a pen in my hand because I have a camera set on the best view of the river: both banks, with a nice

184

foreground of palm fronds, and a little sky. All I need is a large bird in the middle. The distance and exposure are all set. I just have to reach out and push the button. On my neck is another camera, with a much longer lens, which I'll use to try for a closer shot of bird and palm and water. I've got it all worked out. I just need a bird.

Now tiny swallows are darting over the water. But there aren't enough of them to photograph. Too bad, for some fine white powder-puff clouds are nicely outlining the treetops now.

Why doesn't a bird come? An egret. I'll even settle for a stork-billed kingfisher flashing his brilliant blue wings. I'll get it. I have to.

I must do my social report. The Schenkels came to dinner last night, and Sohib outdid himself with the goat. He did two kinds of "sate," which is marinated meat broiled on a bamboo skewer. In one kind he used part of the leg and some liver. I'll have to get the recipe for this, which tastes much like the meat Polynesian restaurants serve with a sweet, dark brown sauce. Then he minced some of the meat, chopped some potatoes in with it, seasoned the mixture, and added (in lieu of regular flour) Bisquick. From the resultant batter he made cakes, which were fried in coconut oil, and came out delicious. For the next dish, he stuffed cucumbers with seasoned chopped meat, then stewed them with tomatoes, very hot chili peppers, and I don't know what else. Last, he made a soup-stew with meat and cabbage and tomatoes that needed only sour cream to make it a substitute for borscht. For dessert I cut up a big papaya (the Schenkels brought me several from Bogor) with some canned litchis.

I must say it was a very nice dinner. Before the Schenkels left I gave Mrs. Schenkel the plastic bag of carrots, scallions, and celery leaves she'd been keeping in my refrigerator. She hasn't one, so unless I keep them for her, her vegetables last only four or five days. I've kept vegetables two weeks if they were well cleaned and dry when put away.

The Schenkels brought me a piece of fresh *tongkol* caught that morning. The Game Department man with them, Widodo, is an ardent fisherman and uses the *Badak* to troll for fish. He caught six yesterday morning, with an average weight of twelve pounds. My piece weighed about two and a half pounds. It was half of one side, filleted. The Schenkels have about ten people to feed. They salt and sun dry what fish they don't eat right away. But I felt they might have spared a little more. We're eight people here. I've given them about five cans of pumpernickel so far, plus several cans of tomato paste and two bottles of wine. But who's counting? And they hinted that I kill the goat for the dinner party. Now Mrs. Schenkel needs faster color film—like my high-speed Ektachrome. Hmmmm!

Dr. Schenkel wasn't too peppy last night although the Lomotil helped. When Talbot and I went over to Peutjang for dinner the evening before Talbot left, Dr. Schenkel made the mistake of showing me how well he skipped rope. People who haven't seen my act with a skipping rope tend not to believe me when I tell them I can do the regular boxer's routine, then go so fast you can't see the rope, then pass the rope twice under while still up in the air (Schenkel did this very well), then make X's without pause, and finally (this always brings down the house) bend my knees, hold my back straight, and in a Russian kazatske dancer's crouch, do X's backward at good speed. I demonstrated for Dr. Schenkel—and that was the end of the skipping.

I'm extremely grateful for the Schenkel's company—when they're here. They aren't here now, for they left on a five-day sortie this morning. With no rain for seven weeks, and no way to track a rhino, they've been going slightly mad. So now they're visiting all the large rivers to measure tracks on the muddy edges. The tracks will tell them something more about the overall rhino population.

When Charles Lindbergh came to the sanctuary in May, he was so taken with it that he asked the Schenkels to allow him to stay with them for a fortnight. They thought he might be some bother, but were amazed at Lindbergh's simplicity. He stayed in an unfinished native-style hut next to their house, slept on a pandanus mat spread on the split-bamboo floor, did his own laundry (one set of khakis was all he had with him), and enjoyed himself thoroughly. Dr. Schenkel, whose first name is Rudolf, told me that on their first walk Lindbergh kept going for six hours without crying uncle. That is something I couldn't have done when I arrived. I'm not so sure I'd want to do it now. What for?

September 16, not quite 6 P.M.

I'm back at the tower, and Radio Antarctica has Lena Horne's "I Give Him All My Love" on, and not bad static. A few minutes ago a song from *Fiddler on the Roof* was announced. I'd get to hear my friend Zero Mostel, I thought, but the record turned out to be by some Australian, singing badly.

No pictures today. Just as the sun dipped behind the trees, a kingfisher and two friends—I think they were sandpipers, large ones—flashed by. Too dark for a good picture. The story of my life.

Anda has just arrived. The canoe is now in the Tjidjung Kulon, and tomorrow at about 7 A.M. we're off.

I'm running out of paper and have to write on both sides.

Just noticed an avocado stone on the table. I remember when

Elin and Jill stuck toothpicks in avocado stones and put them in water to start plants. I didn't know which end was up. I never heard of an avocado as a child.

The other day I planted two avocado stones, three mango stones, and several hundred papaya seeds in the cleared ground around the tower. Some previous philanthropist planted the tops of his pineapples out back, and there are now three young pineapples I'm waiting for more anxiously than Dole. I've planted papayas before, in 1951, in the Congo. Almost everywhere Joan and I stopped for lunch on our way from Stanleyville to Putnam's pygmy headquarters, the Ituri forest, and the Albert National Park, we ate a papaya (obtained from the last town we'd spent the night in), and after we'd finished, I carefully made holes with my stick and planted the seeds. I'm certain they grew—one grove after another, in an area desolate even now with the war still going on there. Tshombe, Mobutu, Mulele, Schramme, Renard, an endless succession of power or lack of it. When I hear what's going on now, I'm very glad I was there this spring and not this fall.

Sunday, September 17, 10:15 A.M.

Back at the tower after paddling up the Tjidjung Kulon.

The Tjidjung Kulon is a beautiful river, almost entirely lined with nipa palms. The nipa has enormous fruit, like the pandanus, and a short stalk of orange flowers. The fruit comes in a cluster larger than a good-sized honeydew melon. I split one seedpod open. Found what looked like a white tennis ball inside; this very hard. The pods float in the water and take root on the banks.

The water was at least two meters deep at medium tide, and I thought the river might be good to swim in—until we came to a steep, muddy bank that a full-grown crocodile had recently slid down. If seeing that croc's track wasn't enough, Anda found the skull of another crocodile—which I collected.

So I didn't go swimming in the Tjidjung Kulon. And I won't. I may, however, try some fishing there, for the river has plenty of small and large fish, including "gerongs" and "talangs." A few minutes ago I gave Anda my fishing line, and he's going to try it in the Tjidjung Kulon later today.

Had to do Polaroids of Suleman, Sanara, Sohib, and Enang this morning; they wanted them to take home to show the folks at Tamandjaja. Sanara, our clown, took a boxing pose.

May go out to a blind soon. May not. I have lots to do to get ready for the hegira to Djakarta tomorrow.

September 17, 2:45 P.M.

In the second of the two new blinds built yesterday between the river blind and the center-field one.

Three of the banteng females came right in front a few minutes ago, but in flat light and against a boring background. Then the mother peahen who once had three chicks came by with only two. I wonder how many she started with. She was very suspicious. The wind was more or less neutral, across both of us, but she caught it too quickly and was gone.

The chicks are so small that it's very difficult to get both of them clear of a low bush. But I know I have one shot in which you can see the mother and both children clearly.

The bantengs are still here. They're on my left now, grazing contentedly. Dull animals. The little one, which has joined them now, has grown quite a bit and is about half again as large as it was last month.

There are a few things I'm looking forward to in Djakarta: a bath in a tub, a very short haircut, and of course, my mail and cables. Also want to be able to send a cable—send one right away instead of waiting ten days for it to be sent. And want to eat in a Chinese restaurant, and to have some people to talk to. But Djakarta is a really dull town. An interesting museum, but

A peahen with two young was extremely nervous passing near the author's blind on the grazing ground.

not one nightclub or dance hall—and I'm far from celibate by nature. Only one bar, in the Hotel Indonesia; full of foreigners.

3:15 P.M. Several gray monkeys have relieved the monotony. They're too far away to photograph, but it's good to know they're here. They walk on all fours and then stop, stand on two legs, and look around. Then they go on. But one has come close enough to photograph.

A crow came and was brushed off by one of the bantengs.

One of a group of monkeys who can the grazing groun, eat the flowers of "sempur" tree.

3:30. Must amend my remarks about the peahen and chicks. They came by again. This time downwind from me, with no reaction. The chicks are very small. Now think it was another hen and two other, younger chicks.

Two of the hens we're keeping at the tower are setting—and also taunting me. One has six eggs, and the other has eleven. We ate the big rooster, but the younger one may have fertilized the eggs. What we'd do with chicks I don't know, but we could certainly use the eggs, which I have not been able to take away. They are small but fresh. I can hardly stand the old chicken eggs we get from Labuan. If you don't open each one separately, you're sure to spoil the lot. At least half are rotten.

September 17, 6 P.M.

Back in the tower having dinner, and the whole banteng crew shows up—old bull, young bull, several cows, and the calf. But almost no light now. And the animals are too wary to stand an approach. Unless you're already in the blind, it's five to one you'll spook them. I did sneak out to the blind once, crawling most of the way. Not tonight. Everything is packed for the voyage.

Sunday, September 24, 9:15 A.M.

Got back to Udjong Kulon Friday and spent yesterday on Peutjang.

Now I'm aboard the *Harini,* on my way to the north end of the peninsula, to a grazing ground and a marsh called Njiur. It's only about two hours away, but I've taken the camping gear and will spend the night. Plan to have the men build a small blind this afternoon, facing the marsh, where many birds come. Then, at dawn, I'll try for an atmosphere shot. I think everyone's tired of great big suns filling the whole page; Schultess, the wonderful Swiss photographer, started this and has been copied *ad nauseam.* But birds flying against a big sun—that could be wonderful. Maybe the shot is just a dream, but I'm going to try for it anyhow.

The mechanic on board is busy twisting a fine piece of wire onto a swivel to which a new large Norwegian fishhook is attached. This wire is a long story. Four times out of five when the men trolled behind the *Harini* a large fish, like a "tongkol," would bite through their monofilament line. What was needed was a wire leader. When I arrived in Djakarta, one of the first things I looked for was the right kind of wire.

I also had to have my visa extended, as it was about to expire, and the Indonesians are very touchy about expired visas. And I needed an exchange of cables with Pat Hunt to find out what was good and what was bad in the film that had so far gotten to New York. I stayed in Djakarta long enough to have a specific list of questions answered. Seems New York is happy with most of the material and especially so with the shots of a rusa and of a peacock which have a "mysterious quality." Wish I knew which shots these were. A "mysterious" picture—of an animal in a dark brooding forest, for example—gives character to a story. One of the shots Pat likes must be of the rusa stag on Peutjang.

Getting back to the story of the wire, Amir Daud and I went to three sports stores and couldn't find any. Finally it occurred to me that a wire guitar string might do, and not knowing which string would be best, I bought two, the second and third strings, of different thickness. A day later—I stayed in Djakarta longer than I originally planned—I thought of the regular Indonesian tuna fishermen. There were several stores at the fishing docks, and in them I found plenty of wire and also some Japanese swivels and Norwegian fishhooks. The men are using them now, trolling, hoping for a strike.

I was so angry when I came on board that I practically held a court martial. Ong Tjibun, I'd learned, had had Anda's rifle when the gear came on board early this morning. There were two shells in the magazine, and Ong managed to charge the weapon and fire it.

Ong tried to tell me that the rifle went off when he put it on deck. But I know the gun, and I also knew both shells were kept in the clip. So there was hell aboard, and I have now taken possession of the gun, although it belongs to the Forestry Department.

On board with me is Ed Barber, a third secretary in the Political Section of the American Embassy. He's a very pleasant young man, about thirty, whom I met at a dinner party in Djakarta. He's keen on camping and the outdoors, and since he had a week leave coming, he asked if he could go to Udjong Kulon with me. I was glad to take him along. For one thing, he speaks fluent Indonesian, and for another, I've been going slightly crazy from being alone.

We left Djakarta on the 22nd at 5 A.M., and it took a total of twenty hours to get to the tower. The car trip from Djakarta to Labuan was normal, even a little fast—three and a half hours —and once in Labuan, I rushed around buying things. Among my purchases were several kilos of squid; some of the squid were the same size as those I buy in New York and cut up in thin slices and deep fry, and the others were tiny and could be eaten whole. I also bought two small "tongkol," because we had no fish in camp. We cooked half the squid and one of the fish on the *Harini* en route. The squid were rolled in a sauce, then fried, and they tasted wonderful. To make the sauce the *Harini* cook used rock salt that he'd crushed in a mortar, sugar, onion, a yellow root called "kunir," tamarind paste, and a little water.

Last night, at the tower, I had nerve enough to try a culinary experiment with the rest of the squid. I dipped the sliced squid in a mixture of duck eggs, Bisquick, salt, and water and then fried it in margarine and olive oil. It was no tempura, but really delicious; with it I served soft lettuce and raw sliced cauliflower. Cauliflower is so perishable here that Indonesians carry each head to market in a separate small, open-meshed basket of a kind specially woven for carrying cauliflower. I cooked the center part of the head of cauliflower last night and left it in its broth for when we get home tomorrow. I plan to make a cheese sauce for it in a double-boiler arrangement on the campfire.

Brought a beautiful collection of fruit and vegetables from Djakarta. I couldn't understand, once I saw the market called Tjikini, why the Schenkels buy their stuff in Bogor or Labuan. There's just no comparison. In addition to beautiful soft lettuce (only one head of which survived), I bought large and tiny cucumbers, two kinds of eggplant, the nicest large tomatoes (the kind you don't mind peeling to eat raw), potatoes large enough for baking, several kinds of onions, including long ones that look like leeks, young celery (which should be excellent for soups), long carrots fat and straight enough to be cleaned easily and without too much waste (most of the carrots from Labuan are so thin and crooked that they're half gone by the time you've got them scraped), red and white cabbage and two kinds of Chinese cabbage, mustard greens (for Chinese soup), enormous red beets, string beans, sweet peas, hot red peppers, ginger, garlic . . . and more. The fruits I bought were as varied as the vegetables, but more exotic. They included three kinds of mangoes, pineapples, grapefruits, avocados, mandarins, lemons, a watermelon, several kinds of bananas, big orange-meated papayas, star apples, rambutans (which have a delicious white pulp, like that of fresh litchi), a jackfruit like those found in the West Indies and Africa, and some foul-smelling durians.

The American ambassador to Indonesia, Marshall Green, whom I saw at lunch during this last visit, told me that he hates durian. He likes cheese, he said, but he doesn't like fruit that smells and tastes like overripe cheese. We were talking about Indonesian fruit, and he went on to tell me about a time he sat next to Sukarno, who was eating durian. Sukarno gouged out a big piece of the fruit with his fingers, put it in front of the ambassador, and said, "Eat it." Green almost gagged getting it down for the U.S.A. whereupon Sukarno gave him another piece for good measure. Ambassador Green ate that one, too.

I hardly needed any canned goods this time, except for a few cans of peaches. Did buy some Indian mango chutney, and a

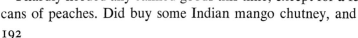

to Malaya, are worth describing. They stand in about twenty feet of water and are built of large, thick bamboo poles. About fifteen feet above the water is a platform some thirty feet square; on the platform is a small shelter. The fishermen on each platform lower a huge net from it into the water, then suspend as many as three strong kerosene lamps a few feet above the net. The fish are attracted to the lights (the fishermen cannot catch anything when there's strong moonlight), and when enough fish are over the net, it is simply hauled up to the platform. I was told that one of these towers can pull in five hundred or more pounds of fish a night. Some of these towers are a mile from shore, and the fishermen paddle out to them in canoes.

In Tamandjaja I saw parts of a tower that was being pre-fabricated on shore. There is no bamboo long enough to go twenty feet into the water and fifteen feet above it, so several poles are spliced together. Men who specialize in this work are brought in to dive to the bottom with the first poles and hammer them into the mud; then they dive again to attach the second poles to the first ones. The entire structure can't be any too strong, for I've seen the remains of more than a few wrecked

Care is taken to land the dugout canoe on a small wave between coral banks.

towers. I was told a big storm always destroys several of the older ones.

We arrived in Tamandjaja after a run of six hours from Labuan, then had to round up the four men the *Harini* had left there on its way out. Harum came to say hello, and I gave him the clothing I'd bought in Djakarta for his new baby girl, Elioti. Enang arrived with a big black goat, which was going to cost me 1,000 rupiahs (150 to the dollar now). I didn't want such a large goat (the last one had been small), or such an expensive one (the last had cost 600 rupiahs), but I took it along, making Enang very happy. He originally asked for 1,050 rupiahs, and I told him 1,000 was my limit, and if he wanted to, he could cut off an ear to bring the price down. This was a big laugh.

We got to Peutjang after midnight and to the tower at 1 A.M. The last part of the *Harini* trip was very windy and very cold. The tower seemed like home. It's extraordinary how one can become attached to a place—familiar surroundings, possessions . . . continuity. Ed and I had some drinks, then I fixed up a mat and air mattress for him on the floor near the window.

Monday, September 25

It is about noon and Ed and I are camped on the northern tip of the peninsula, near the Tjinjiur. This river flows sluggishly through the Njiur, a marsh near the sea that attracts many birds. We landed south of here yesterday and walked an hour and a half along the shore, for there was just too much surf to take a chance on landing closer to our target. We pitched the big tent near the shore, looked for birds, which were scarce, and then had a long swim before dinner.

Ed and I ran down to the shore after dinner. It was still light, when Enang came and told us there was a crocodile swimming offshore. All we could see were the nostrils above water and, at about two hundred yards, not worth even trying to photograph. Ed and I lost interest in any further swimming there, although the beast left almost at once.

This morning we were at the marsh at dawn. But again there were almost no birds, so we returned to camp and had breakfast. Then we tried again—and I goofed.

Just as the trail through the bushes and trees opens up on the marsh, a flock of perhaps two dozen white egrets sprang into flight—before I was set. We had no recourse but to go back to camp, have some tea, and give the egrets a chance to settle down.

After about an hour we went again, and this time didn't spook the birds. They were farther upstream, white notes on a deep green tree. Every once in a while they left the upper branches to swirl around like gliders in a narrow canyon. I'd chosen a place in low-branched trees with trailing vines and was able to get pictures of the birds in space, each bird in its own frame of very out-of-focus, light green, oddly shaped leaves. One shot is entirely covered by these lacy patterns, with birds scattered at random throughout. It should be a magnificent picture, especially when compared with an ordinary shot of birds and sky. The marsh had—and some of the other shots show—areas of light-struck ripply water accented by light green masses of algae.

There were other birds, like cormorants and sandpipers, but my real target was the white egrets, the showiest possible birds in this setting. Even when they're still, their arched necks lend them an air of excitement and movement. Ed and I gave them one or two disturbances so I could catch their flight; then we

Effendy Abdoessoeki, a young biology teacher from Pandung, replaced Sinaga as my guide and interpreter.

came back to camp for lunch. When the egrets have had time to settle again, we'll go back for another try.

September 25, 5:30 P.M.

On the *Harini,* returning to the tower. Had a very good afternoon.

After lunch, Ed Barber, Anda, Effendy, and I began to follow the river upstream, for the egrets had left the trees on the banks and moved inland to Njiur's marshy meadows. The meadows, which are now covered with bright green plants about eight to twelve inches high, look rather like the salt hay meadows found in coastal marshes in Maine and elsewhere.

We found the egrets in a good-sized meadow. We also found four mature bantengs, two bulls and two cows, feeding near each other—and a group of five young peacocks, which marched off to the left. Then, while I was crawling toward the bantengs, using the cover of a fallen tree to hide my approach, a line of five fairly large pigs, one behind the other, crossed within ten yards of me. I had the telephoto in my hands, so I could only get four in one shot.

The egrets were on the far edge of the meadow, but unfortunately they were too far to the left to include in a frame with the bantengs unless I used an extreme wide angle, which would have rendered the birds as specks on the film. It was wonderful to see the birds sitting in the scarce brown fronds atop two crazy palm trees, the trunks of which spiraled like Byzantine columns, forming a very suitable perch for these elegant birds. I did some pictures of the egrets leaving one of these trees without any frame in the foreground. I had not made a dawn shot of the egrets or a shot with a great big sun, but I wasn't too sorry.

There's a saying that history doesn't repeat itself—or is it that lightning doesn't strike twice in the same place? Anyhow, I know that photographic situations rarely recur. Last year in Tanzania our ABC film crew found a good group of large flamingos on a salt lake. I then went out at dawn, took a compass bearing on the sunrise, and staked a position from which to try to get the birds in front of the sun as it rose over the horizon. The next day we were at the staked position at sunrise and made a stunning piece of film showing the birds leaving the lake, their great long legs trailing behind them as they lifted into the air from a takeoff run of what seemed to be at least fifty feet. The way they sort of shoved the water behind them as they took off reminded me of how a seaplane, its engine full out, hits the waves, gets up on a step, and, finally, becomes airborne. Each spurt of water was back lighted by a pink sun. I made many photographs, one of which is among the best I've ever made

erleaf:
ldlife was plentiful
Njiur. Egrets perch
treetops overlook-
the marsh, where
ur wild pigs walk in
gle file.

anywhere. It's certainly my best bird picture.

No situation here resembling that with the flamingos. But I think one of my shots of egrets through the abstract curtain of leaves should do. It looked almost like a Tiffany glass lampshade when I took it.

When it was time to go, we started following the riverbank again—and walked right into a full-grown monitor lizard sunning himself on the gravel. I hit him twice (photographically) with the 300mm lens, and then he slid off into the water. His crawl stroke was something. He made it across the narrow river so fast that I could hardly focus. This really completed my fauna in a big way.

After we'd walked the hour and a half southward to where the *Harini* was waiting for us (and after Anda and Effendy were aboard and all the gear had been loaded), Ed Barber and I looked around very carefully for crocodiles and, not seeing any, decided to swim out to the boat.

It was beautiful—clean, cool green water with just a few big waves to get through before a calm water swim of about five hundred feet. I had to sidestroke, overhand, and then to backstroke to make it, but I did the distance without stopping— which showed me I'm in pretty good condition for a change. Those long marches have helped, and being ten pounds lighter helps, too.

Just stopped to watch one of the crewmen pull in an enormous king mackerel ("tenggiri" in Indonesian) weighing, I'd guess, about fifteen pounds. It's a real beauty, of silver with dark blue streaks on top. Everyone's very pleased, for this fish has fine white meat and is considered one of the best around.

6:20 P.M. I was given the choice of the head or tail half of the mackerel; the crew was to get the other half. I chose the head, much to the delight of Sohib, who asked me for it. Although most Americans don't touch the fish head, I like it. So do the Eskimos who consider it such a delicacy that only the men get a chance at it. Maybe the women get some now, but they didn't when I visited the Mackenzie River delta in the forties.

Tuesday, September 26, 9 A.M.

Ed Barber and I are in the center-field blind in front of the tower. He is anxious to get some pictures of wildlife, but unfortunately his only camera is a Canonette, a good camera with a normal lens. Any animal would have to be close as your wife posing for a snapshot in order to be recognizable. A four times magnification—a 200mm lens, as compared to the normal 50mm—is the minimum one can use on wildlife. This is about the power of a pair of opera glasses.

A monitor lizard is surprised sunbathi. at the edge of the marsh and takes o. the first camera cli

208

So far I haven't said anything more about Saturday, first day back in Udjong Kulon, than that the day was spent on Peutjang. I probably have a block about it, because it was a very sad day. But I must write about it now.

Ed, Effendy, Anda, Enang, and I went to Peutjang arriving about 9 A.M. Saturday on the *Harini*. I needed a better shot of the wild pigs; Pat Hunt had said, and I agreed, that the beautiful trees of Peutjang, many with heavily buttressed trunks, would do nicely as a background. While going to the blind we came across several big male rusa deer which meant we probably wouldn't see any later (somehow the alarm seems to spread). They were too far away to photograph, although Ed was very excited. We also came across some pigs. They also were too far off to get any shots.

The first blind gave me quite a turn. The upper half of a tree had blown down next to it, and a very heavy branch had smashed one side. Not a cozy feeling at all.

After I'd inspected the damaged blind, Ed, Effendy, the two trackers, and I went on to the second blind and had our lunch while waiting for things to settle down in the area. Just as we were finishing, a female barking deer ran by, but rather strangely. Her front end was lower than the rest of her. I made about three pictures, and then Anda said she was probably injured and asked if I would allow him and Enang to try to run her down and capture her. I agreed.

Within five minutes the trackers were being heralded back by the piteous cries of the deer, which was slung around Enang's neck in exactly the same posture as that of the deer in the famous bronze statue from Benin.

She was not injured, but had been born malformed. Both of her front legs were too short, and terribly twisted. There are no predators on Peutjang except pythons, or an animal like this would never have survived its youth. I made a bed of soft leaves to place her on, and Ed and Effendy held her down—Ed holding her rear legs together and Effendy taking her neck until Enang and Anda could quickly fence off the buttresses of a huge tree the trunk of which formed one wall, and a desirable photographic background. Touches of light were edging the buttresses, and this would have been very effective.

*Close-up of the
of a barking dee
shows an unusu
gland underneat
eye.*

It turned out that Enang and Anda really needn't have bothered with the fences, disguised with tree branches, for when Ed and I put the poor animal into the set, she couldn't get up. She lay there, sides heaving and eyes half shut. I tried to take some photographs of her with her head resting on a low root, but having her head moved, even just a few inches, was plainly too much for her. She was obviously suffering from shock. I gave her some water but she took very little.

210

In about an hour she simply died, while we watched. We went back to the tower very depressed. Even though she was a hopeless cripple, we'd killed her.

Often you see attractive subjects through a telephoto lens, and you know they won't photograph. For example, on Peutjang part of a rusa often appeared in a spot of bright sunshine, with the rest of the animal in pitch-black shadow; no color film can accommodate this wide difference of exposure. There are also objects too far away to photograph. On our way back from the blind we came across a pair of deer, a full-grown male and

his girl friend. She had to be that because he was putting on quite a show for her. Demonstrating his strength, he tore at some low bushes with his big antlers, dropping his head very low, getting his antlers under the branches, and then by lifting his head forcibly, tearing up the foliage. When he'd done this for several minutes, he pranced off with his head completely

festooned in green, like some ancient Greek god. Of course I tried to photograph this. But even with my 300mm lens, which gives a magnification of six, the images were barely large enough to show what they were doing. A still photograph would be very unlikely to give people the pleasure I had watching them —in motion.

9:45 A.M. A young peacock is right in front of the blind now but too far away for even the 500mm—unless a group of trees gives it a nice frame. Ed made one shot, but I'm afraid that it will take a magnifying glass to find the bird. I did one or two with the 500 to give him later on. He's been reading Evelyn Waugh's *Men at Arms* and keeps holding back his laughter. I must get this book when he's finished.

September 26, 5:20 P.M.

Back at the tower now. An hour ago Ed and I made a hundred-yard dash—fairly quietly—from the center-field blind to the new one in left field to try to catch a group of bantengs that had come out of the forest and headed toward the new blind. Before risking the move, I waited until the bantengs were hidden from our view, which meant they couldn't see us. We made it. But the bantengs were so close—only about ten yards from us— that when the wind shifted, after only a few minutes, off they went. I tried a running shot, which may turn out to be my first-wild-looking picture of these domestic-looking animals.

Wednesday, September 27, 11:40 A.M.

I'm in the second blind on Peutjang. Anda, Enang, and I crossed over on the *Harini* at nine this morning.

Had to play doctor before I could leave. Last night Ong Tjibun came to the tower to complain that he'd been vomiting after meals for the last two days. I gave him three antibiotic (Panalba) capsules (for a day) and some Bisodol. I also put him on light food and supplied him with some egg noodles and bouillon cubes. The Indonesians eat food that can be matched with the hottest Indian curry. Then I had a look at the *Harini's* water supply—which I found in an old oil drum with a filthy interior. I had the crew empty it, scrub it with a strong solution of potassium permanganate (part of my first-aid kit), and then fill it with fresh water. Ong is better today—no more vomiting —but when he showed up at the tower this morning, I gave him three more Bisodols, one for after each meal.

Two *Harini* crewmen came along with Ong this morning. They wanted me to have a look at rashes on their thighs and buttocks. Each of these men got a squeeze of zinc ointment on his index finger, and instructions about what to do.

When we got to Peutjang I stopped to see Mrs. Schenkel and

The captured barking deer suffered deep shock and never regained its feet before lying there.

apologize. She sent over bananas yesterday morning, and with them a note inviting Ed and me to dinner last night. The bananas—and note—arrived while I was out, and without mentioning it, Amir put the bananas on top of the note, which I didn't find until this morning. Very frustrating. But Mrs. Schenkel invited us again for tonight. I accepted, but I don't know when Ed will be back. Since he's already seen Peutjang, I sent him with two guides to walk across the peninsula to the Tjibunar. It's just a three-hour walk, but he's also going to walk eastward to see the surf on the south coast. I hope he gets back early enough to join me, as the Schenkels usually eat at five.

So far there's not much action around the blind, but there was plenty on the way here. There were so many rusa deer between the beach and the first blind (which is unusable, since I haven't bothered to have it repaired) that Anda and I left Enang in the second blind and backtracked, carrying between us three Nikons, two with Kodachrome and one with high-speed Ektachrome, and a tall forked stick to rest the 200 and 300mm lenses; the third camera had the 105 on for slow exposures. Most of the pictures I made were at 1/15 or 1/30 second with the 200 and would have been almost impossible to do with a completely hand-held camera.

Had some luck, but not enough. In doing pictures of wildlife a clear shot of an animal is just not good enough. It's the atmosphere of the forest and the animal—together—that conveys an idea or emotion. I had just one good chance. I spotted a large tree trunk washed with sunlight and waited nearby for a male rusa to walk past and silhouette his great antlers against it. One did, but not in the perfect position, for only a few feet out of the picture was a great strangler fig, and just beyond it, a twisted vine as thick as your thigh climbing up into the trees. Either the strangler or the vine would have completed the feeling perfectly, but you can't move the deer to line up the right background. You can't move yourself either, for deer have great eyes and spot the slightest movement. They even seem to see movements that are behind them.

1:10 P.M. Still not a single animal or large bird. And it's very hot here in the blind. The sun has found a hole through the leaf cover over our heads and is about to bake us. I had to break silence to tell Anda and Enang to cut some long poles, put them across the top of the blind, then pile leafy branches on them. Sun in Indonesian is "matahari." Who would have guessed the use of this word for the adopted name of a famous female spy during World War I?

I'm especially after wild pigs today (Pat Hunt particularly asked for a close-up of one), but I haven't seen any. Usually the woods are full of them. Perhaps the line of four pigs I made

214

at Njiur Monday will do. Think I'll go back to Njiur tomorrow, return the following day. It's the best spot I've found so far in Udjong Kulon for a variety of subjects, and I've yet to milk it dry.

Sunday, or perhaps Monday (October 1 or 2), I'll be off for Djakarta again. Intend to do some photography at the zoo, which has pythons, gibbons, crocodiles, and a leopard of the species found here in the sanctuary. It also has a flying lizard. The zoo photography should take about five days, until about the 7th. Then perhaps a week for Time-Life Books on Indonesian food for their "Foods of the World" series will give me a chance to get to Sumatra, central Java (including the great temples like Borobudur and Prambanan), and, of course, Bali. This is the only way to see a place—doing something that involves you with it. Also I'll get a minimum of $1,250 for the week: more if my photographs fill over $1,250 worth of pages. I should be back at the sanctuary on October 15, ready to wait for a rhino.

Held a short staff meeting this morning and asked who wanted to stay with Amir during my absence. Two men are needed to mind the tower. Sohib volunteered to stay if I'd take fifty liters of rice to his family—so he wouldn't have to worry. Sohib has only four children, and this is about a hundred pounds of rice—for two weeks! I agreed. I'm giving Sohib, and Amir too, full salary; Anda, Enang, Suleman, and Sanara are going home to Tamandjaja at half pay. I asked Sohib—with Sutrisno translating—what he'd want if *I* stayed at the tower with him and sent Amir home. "Double," he answered with a smile. Sutrisno will go back to work with Dr. Schenkel.

When I get back I'll be spending forty-hour stretches on a platform up in some trees that move with the wind. I'm not exactly looking forward to it, but it will be my last chance to get a clear shot at a Java rhino. These animals are really rare. At one time they were spread over most of Java; now Udjong Kulon is the last refuge for the perhaps two dozen or so that are left.

My plan now is to set up a camp near the Tjiembang, on the western end of the sanctuary, with Sohib, Suleman, Effendy, and Enang (leaving Amir and Sanara at the tower) and to go to the blind for two-day stretches. Every other evening I'll come out for a decent dinner and bath, and just to walk around. In the blind with me I'll have Anda, who can smell a rhino before he can see it.

What my time limit will be is hard to tell. I truly wanted to be back in New York by October 1. That was before I knew about the total absence of rain this season, and before I improvised the book assignment. I could have planned the trip to Bali as a week's vacation, but I really don't enjoy going to a place like that and being just a sightseer.

This delay will make problems for me on my return home. I'm supposed to go to Los Angeles to complete the photography for *The Hollywood Style,* the big book Arthur Knight and I are doing. I cannot delay that beyond November 15, because the book is to go to press the first of the year. I'm now setting November 1 as the date I'll get to New York. On the way, I'll stop in Tokyo for a day or two to see the newspaper people who have invited me to have a show of my color photographs there. Their letter offered round-trip fare from New York and $1,000 as the fee for two lectures, but it didn't go into the question of my living expenses in Tokyo. Making color prints wasn't discussed either. At commercial prices this could cost $10,000— an amount I'm not about to spend. Chang, who's *Time-Life* correspondent in Tokyo and also a columnist for the sponsoring newspaper, wants to arrange for a simultaneous exhibition of my water colors at a Tokyo art gallery. I feel that this painting show may not work out too well, since I'm not a very modern painter. I paint on a flat piece of paper; nothing sticks out of it. There are no paste-ups, no collages, no glues; there's just water color and sometimes India ink. Worse still, the work is influenced by traditional Japanese painting. Imitation may be the sincerest form of flattery, but . . .

The paintings are not Japanese paintings, and they can be recognized as mine. Still, I don't know. A few years ago I brought a portfolio to Tokyo with me, and Chang and his friends liked the paintings in it very much. In fact, Chang brought the curator of the Tokyo Museum of Western Art to see them, and one was added to the museum's collection. This year I sent one to H. Shirahama, president of Nikon, who wrote me that it is now hanging in his office. I also sent one to Jerrold Schechter, the chief of *Time-Life's* Tokyo bureau. He's a wonderful man with a great family and was very hospitable when I visited Tokyo earlier this year. I usually don't give paintings away, as this tends to cheapen them.

1:55. I've been writing away because I'm sure nothing will come to the blind today. I may strike it and sortie out again with Anda to try for whatever animals I can find. I'll wait here until 2:30, and if nothing shows, then out we go.

2:05. Just made a terrible mistake. Had a small flask of red wine in my pack to go with my lunch of cold fried fish, rice, and a cucumber. Tried diluting the last of the wine with boiled water. It was ghastly. What works here with tea or whisky doesn't work with wine. Not at all.

At least it's gotten nice and cool here since Anda and Enang threw up the roof.

I'm just sitting here, Buddha fashion, on a pandanus mat, looking at Anda and Enang. Enang keeps falling asleep instead of watching his side of the blind. Since I don't expect any animals to blunder by, I've been letting him sleep for a while and then waking him. The trackers are as bad as I am about not sitting still.

Now Anda's asleep too. I'll have to watch both sides. He and Enang—and all the men—are wonderful simple people. At least, this is how they seem to me. I was very pleased when Sohib jokingly asked for double pay if he had to stay over just with me. I haven't yet given the men the toys I bought for their children when I was in Djakarta. I'll do that Sunday or Monday, just before we leave. It should be something.

Thursday, September 28, 10 A.M.

On the *Harini* on the way to Njiur. We'll again land about an hour and a half walk away. I'd thought about going to Njiur's shore and having a look at the surf from the *Harini,* but last night when Ed and I were having dinner with the Schenkels (Ed made it back to the tower in plenty of time to reach Peutjang before five), Mrs. Schenkel casually mentioned that their canoe had turned over twice there. I'd much rather make the walk than risk a canoe upset.

Sanara, my best porter, is along today, so we can make the portage in one trip instead of the two it took Sunday. Amir is with us, as he's never seen Njiur and will be restricted to the tower when I leave for Djakarta. Ed, who's also along, will be leaving the sanctuary Saturday. He's going on the *Badak* with the Schenkels so he can be sure of being in his office Monday morning.

I haven't decided yet whether I'll go Sunday or Monday. It depends on the material I can find on this trip. We'll be back at the tower tomorrow evening.

Effendy is staying at the tower, since he's just been to Njiur; Ong is keeping him company. Before we left this morning, I cooked chicken in the pot (the two chickens I used were killed yesterday) and gave Effendy and Ong a good portion for their lunch. I also gave them a rather odd piece of food: the liver of a six-foot shark the *Harini's* crew caught last night with my new hook and wire. The crew sent the liver, which is very large, and considered a delicacy, as a token of appreciation for the hook and wire. I knew about shark-fin soup, but I'd never heard of eating the heart.

Very gray and cloudy this morning. It could almost rain, but I'm afraid I'm not that lucky. I have never before hoped so much for rain. It's so humid here without it that I cannot imagine what it will be like when it really comes.

We are at the Njiur campsite again. The sun is almost down, and I have a Scotch and water in my left hand as I'm writing this page. I'm utterly exhausted. Getting here took almost two hours of climbing over sharp coral reefs in the broiling sun. As soon as we arrived I stripped, ran into the surf, and in trying to argue right of way with a sharp branch, got a bad scratch on my right shoulder. The trees stick out over the reef—and if you don't duck under the branches—and at the same time hop over fallen trees—you're in for it. Just like an obstacle course at over 100° F.

Anda and I hastened to the river. A single white egret fluttered away on our arrival, but I didn't care. I was particularly after "babi," pig in Indonesian, and soon two different ones came so close to me that I could have thrown my Nikon and hit them. Got real close-ups, but in bad light.

When we reached the big meadow I spotted a group of pigs at the far end. We ran through the woods at the edge of the meadow to reach a good vantage point, which turned out to be a perfect one. About fifteen pigs, including small ones, came right across the camera at about a hundred feet. I made a whole roll with different lenses and shot on two cameras, which was indeed fortunate, as I had a failure on one box. [Failure discovered when I returned to base camp where I cleaned and inspected all equipment after each sortie. The shutter had slowed down considerably and this can be heard at slow speeds. Did not fix, but shelved this camera.] Something I learned a long time ago: always shoot important subjects with two different cameras and at least two lenses. Then you're fairly safe, even in rugged terrain like this.

Also did a group of five peacocks this afternoon. And three of the birds obliged me by posing in the top of one of the palms with a Byzantine trunk. Monday the tops of these palms had a few brown fronds—or at least I thought they did. This afternoon the tops were bare. Around the base of each of these trees was a jungle of fallen fronds, all edged with huge teeth, like those on a lumberjack's saw. The trees must change their foliage each year; very unusual for palms.

Ed and I are going to have chicken in the pot tonight. I made it this morning before leaving. We're also having Rosé d'Anjou, which I'll chill by wrapping the bottle in a wet towel and putting it where the breeze can evaporate the water and thus cool the wine.

Sunday, October 1, 9:30 A.M.

On the *Harini* on the way to Tamandjaja and then Labuan. Today's a real howler, with the water the roughest it's been since my arrival. To make matters worse, the ship has prop trouble and can only go at reduced speed. The estimate for the trip is about thirteen hours instead of eleven.

We left at 8 A.M. to go to the northwest corner of Peutjang so I could get one more crack at the fruit bats. The trees were loaded with them, but the water was too rough to try to land anyone to scare them into the air. Anda sacrificed the only bullet he had left for his rifle, and the crew and passengers—including seven people from the lighthouse who needed passage to Labuan—beat with sticks on every pot and pan aboard. But we succeeded in raising only some of the bats. So I'll have to try again when I return for the rhino vigil.

Yesterday I wasn't so sure we were going to be able to leave at all, for when I went to the *Harini* to make final arrangements for the trip, Ong had a very nasty dagger in his hand and was threatening both the captain and the mechanic. I disarmed him, but I still don't know what the fight was about. Usually it's women or money, and we have no women here.

Yesterday was too full a day. Early in the morning, after I saw off the *Badak* with the Schenkels and Ed aboard, I went for a last look at the rhino blind, which I've now named Badak House. I'm glad I went, as I discovered that part of the roof had blown off. Since the roof had to be fixed anyway, I also wanted it made rainproof. Anda, Enang, Suleman, and Sanara went to work on this, and Effendy and I decided to leave them and go down the hill to the coast, normally a thirty-minute walk, and then back to the tower.

I thought the trail down the hill was an easy one to follow. Effendy led the way. And we were very lucky finally to get to the coast—after three hours of being lost.

Some people are color blind. Me, I'm totally without a sense of direction. For example, in the Time & Life Building, where I have my office, there are two elevator banks—east and west—with cars that go to the twenty-eighth floor. When I get off the elevator, I can go either right or left; one side is the darkroom, and the other is where the photographers are. If there wasn't a burlap wall on one side and a white wall on the other, I'd never know which way to turn. This after ten years or so.

When Effendy and I started back to the tower yesterday we left all our gear except three cameras and lenses and one canteen partially filled with cold tea for the men to bring back. I put the snakebite kit in my pocket but did not take my compass. I'll never leave it behind again. I also left my sheath knife and matches. I never imagined we could get lost.

What happened was that our trail crossed an old one of Dr. Schenkel's going off in another direction, and Effendy, who was following cut-off branches and bushes, went onto that one.

When thirty minutes had gone by and we hadn't reached the coast, we looked a little closer at our path and noticed that the cuts were weeks old. We then knew we'd goofed.

We thought we'd just go back to where we left our trail. But this didn't work at all. Dr. Schenkel had cut more than one trail, and we kept running into forks—without having any idea where we were or which branch to take. So we were stuck.

It was only 1 P.M. and too early to use the sun accurately for a bearing.

So that I'd at least know if we were going in a circle, and also to help our men find us, I began to cut arenga palms along our way, breaking the fronds near the middle and leaving the front end dangling like a flag. When we came to a fork I left a green branch on the ground at the start of the trail we took. Luckily I still had my pocketknife, which was attached to a lanyard on my belt.

At 2 P.M. I was able to line up a pair of trees with the sun, wait until it had moved and thus establish which way was west.

Just now a group of about ten porpoises flashed by the *Harini,* looping above the waves. But the porpoises were gone before any camera could be unpacked.

To come back to the forest. Once I established west, and from it the other directions, we started to work our way north, hoping to find our men, who were to go to the shore in that direction after they'd finished repairing the blind. As we walked, I was able to find an occasional patch of open sky, and since the prevailing wind is constantly from the south, I could check our direction against cloud movements.

There wasn't enough tea in the canteen to do anything more than wet our mouths. And we were both hot. I was beginning to think about how we could prepare ourselves to spend the night in the forest. I knew we'd be found, because I kept marking our trail with palm flags, but I didn't know how long it would take. Nor was I at all certain we'd find our own way out.

Dr. Schenkel had come into this area from the south shore, and this was where we didn't want to go. Moving due west would have brought us to the lighthouse, but the highest hill on the peninsula was west of us—and in the way. So we had to go south. Our problem was that Schenkel's paths often went west. We couldn't move south without a trail, as we had no machete to cut our way, and without one, the forest is impassable.

The hours between twelve-thirty and three were very uncomfortable. Effendy has had a total of three months' field experience. Luckily I've had many years of it. Talbot and I had joked about a printed card he'd found in my first-aid kit. Its topic was what to do if you're lost in the woods.

Effendy and I were very happy when, finally, the trail we were on crossed our own trail—the one we'd started out on— and we at last reached the coast. We didn't have to sleep on arenga branches and worry about leopards and snakes and no food or water or cover. The men were very amused to hear that we had been lost. At first they'd thought that I'd been taking pictures. Only a rhino would have opened my camera.

There was a canteen of water in the gear I'd left for the men to carry. Effendy and I gulped it down. I will never do that path without our men. And I will always carry a compass.

Just finished a sumptuous lunch.

I don't know if I know anyone who'd improvise, scrounge, and make do in my fashion. Last night when I came home from my forest foolishness I had a big gin and tonic and a hot shower— a nice start. Then I made a vinaigrette sauce—olive oil, American cider vinegar (wish it had been wine vinegar, and French tarragon), garlic, ReaLemon, salt and freshly ground pepper, a pinch of mustard and brown sugar. Two of the avocados I'd bought in Djakarta were left; I felt them, chose one, and stuffed it with most of the jar of tiny Greenland shrimp. I ate this with some of the vinaigrette sauce. Then I had "tenggiri" (the best fish here) in a dish called "pindag ketjap"—fish stewed with cabbage, tomatoes, onion, carrot, and "ketjap," a sauce made from soybeans and highly spiced. This with rice.

While fixing dinner I poached two slices of the same fish with celery salt, onion, and carrots using half water, half Chablis. In another pot I boiled some quartered potatoes, adding one onion for flavor. The fish and potatoes went into the refrigerator until this morning, when I made up a jar of potato salad for the lunch basket, adding the shrimp that were left to the potatoes and some diced raw onion. I packed the fish in two plastic bags, the carrots in another, and then I put the three bags into an empty coffee can and the coffee can into the lunch basket. I still had one avocado and the rest of the vinaigrette sauce in a small jar, which went into the lunch basket, too.

The sumptuous lunch I just finished consisted of fish, potato salad, and avocado with a '62 Chablis from Saccone and Speed in London, a sliced mango, and four squares of Swiss bittersweet chocolate. I couldn't have done better at Maxim's.

Very difficult to write clearly—the *Harini* is pitching so. Want to describe where I am, which is where I had my lunch— and is not at all like Maxim's.

Midships on the *Harini* is a deckhouse about six feet wide, nine feet long, and seven feet high. At the back of it is a sleeping platform about three feet high. There is a door on each side forward of the sleeping platform, and there are four windows. I'm sitting on the right side of the platform, my feet hanging from the edge and supported on a wooden crate. On the left is a weather-beaten Indonesian lady who's trying to sleep; her knees are drawn up sharply, and under her head is a bundle of clothes wrapped up in a nice brown imitation batik. Between us is her small son, trying to sleep in the crook of her arm.

The back of the platform is filled with my camera cases, which are dry and cool there. The crew's possessions—old clothes, lamps, plaited grass sacks, old bottles of "ketjap," tin cups, a shortwave radio, and a two-foot-long Indonesian flag —are all over the place. Near the flag about a dozen very long peacock feathers; these, which are incredibly beautiful, belong to Ong.

The mother and child are asleep now. The father is outside with the rest of the passengers.

It's just too rough to write.

Monday, October 2, 4 P.M.

Just a quick note. Finally arrived at Labuan at 10:30 last night. No water in the channel to ride up the river, and too rough for a canoe landing on shore. So Ong obligingly ran the *Harini* almost up onto the beach so the passengers could wade in. Meanwhile the crew jumped overboard and fastened an anchor and line on each side of the boat so it wouldn't turn broadside to the surf.

The car had come for me. But the driver had given up waiting and returned to Djakarta at 9 P.M. So I slept on a mattress on the floor at Djuhari's house.

The car returned at 8:30 this morning. We arrived in Djakarta at 1 P.M. This is being written at the Hotel Indonesia there. A day and a half of rather unpleasant traveling.

Tuesday, October 24, 11:55 A.M.

Back on the *Harini,* bound for Udjong Kulon. Left Djakarta at 7 A.M. with Effendy. Have been away from the sanctuary over three weeks. Left on October 1, after it had become obvious that the monsoon was really late this year. Photographers get sick and tired of hearing people say, "If only you were here last year," or " . . . last month," or ". . . yesterday"; "If only you'd still be here tomorrow."

Last year the monsoon came in September. But this is the driest summer in years—just for me. The Javanese rhinoceros, my photographic target, is one of the rarest animals in existence; only two dozen or so are still extant—all in Udjong Kulon. Tracking a rhino is fairly simple when the ground is wet, since its footstep is about eight inches across. But when there's no rain, and no ground wet enough to take a print, you haven't any chance at all.

If it rained a little while I was gone, I'll probably try tracking. If it is raining, then I can go into the blind and wait for a rhino to come to the mud wallow it overlooks. The meteorological forecast from Djakarta was rather glum: no monsoon until mid-November. But I'm going back anyway, for a last chance.

Can't stay beyond November 3 because *Life* will close the year-end issue November 6. My film can be in New York on the 6th if I get it to Djakarta on the 3rd. More than that I can't do, although I have thought seriously of staying longer, *Life* or not. It's a personal matter: I want a rhino.

Our gear being landed near the mouth of the Tjigenter included three chickens to supplement canned food.

But, no. I'm just a working photographer—with a book to finish on Hollywood before January 1. From the sublime to the ridiculous. But that's what journalism is all about.

I've had a rather fine three weeks. I was repeating myself in

Udjong Kulon, doing the same jungle and the same animals over and over again. I needed to change my perspective. Also, wanted to do some close-ups of animals that had eluded my camera in the sanctuary. These I did at the Djakarta zoo.

I see no reason why the photographic coverage for a scientific or instructive story on wildlife shouldn't be augmented, if necessary, with detail shots made nearby, provided the species and setting are the same. The closest I came to a good-sized crocodile in the sanctuary was two hundred yards, so why not do pictures at the zoo? Of course you want to maintain the mood and feeling of the story, so you try to take such pictures under the most natural conditions possible. Simulating a setting can involve rather a tremendous amount of labor. For example, in order to simulate the banks of the sanctuary's rivers, it was necessary to have a score of men dig a segment of "river" about two feet deep and twenty feet wide. They did this by enlarging

A half-grown crocodile at the Djakarta Zoo is the same species that is found at Udjong Kulon.

a ditch near the zoo pond in which three crocodiles lived. I had a truck bring in a dozen nipa palms like those found on the banks of the sanctuary's rivers, and not only did I plant these but I also broke some of the lower stems to trail into the water just as nipa stems do for real. When the setting was ready, about ten men with long bamboo poles pushed and prodded the crocs to come toward my camera, which was deliberately placed— again to simulate reality—so I'd be shooting at the crocs through a leafy screen.

October 24, 12:45 P.M.

Stopped writing when the *Harini* cook handed me a plateful of fresh squid cut in rings and fried quickly in coconut oil. Delicious! I bought the squid in the Labuan market before shoving off. They're baby squid, about three or four inches long from the tips of their tentacles to the bottom of the tube that forms their body, and they're the most! Never saw these small ones in Italy, which was where I first learned about deep-fried squid. In Genoa many restaurants serve a dish of squid, small pieces of whitebait, shrimp, and almost anything else that happened to be in the market that morning; they call it Fruit of the Sea.

To continue the discussion of honesty in photography in depth would take a small volume. Some years ago I wrote a paper on this subject for a nationwide nonsectarian conference on ethics held at the Jewish Theological Seminary. There were seminars in government, science, education, art, etc. I learned a lot about this subject by having to think it out for the first time.

Photographers usually do what they think is right professionally, and I do this almost instinctively. For example, when I photograph a movie star, especially an older female, I obscure the wrinkles by pouring soft light into them from as close to the camera as possible; this washes out the shadows that delineate the lines. I also use diffusion filters, for a softer effect. Is this dishonest? Is the unnecessarily cruel photograph of the Duke and Duchess of Windsor that was published in a book an honest picture because it shows every wrinkle and line in their faces?

There are many obvious ways to distort any image. Viewpoint can be chosen to distort; for example, a short person shot from a very low angle will look taller than he really is. Filters can also be used to distort, changing, for example, a light sky to one that's almost black. Using color film so inaccurate that tests with four different types produce four different color effects is bound to result in distortion. I think that photography is a personal expression, and that each man must determine for himself what is or is not an honest picture.

Getting a bit rough on the *Harini* now. Just looked back toward Labuan Bay. Discovered a volcano-shaped mountain towering over the delicate fringe of tall coconut palms that marks the coastal plain. Most of it was covered with clouds on my previous trips. Elegant sailing canoes, some with two sails— I'd seen these canoes before, too—were skimming in to shore as the *Harini* left the bay.

I checked on the recent weather in Labuan: five small rains in three weeks. But a game warden who'd just come from the sanctuary said not a drop had fallen there. I will not call this diary *Rain and the Rhino*.

It's surprising to me how good I feel to be on the *Harini* again, heading back to the sanctuary. I've already had almost two months of it. But nothing there is really repetitious. The attempt to photograph it might be. But the splendor of nature is unique in Udjong Kulon's rain forest, in the occasional savannas with which the forest is dotted, in the sanctuary's marshy coastal plains, and in the clear blue and green of the sea around the sanctuary. And then there are the animals.

One of the animals I did not see was a gibbon—a long-armed ape which lives entirely in the trees. How do you photograph a gibbon in a zoo and achieve reality? You choose a group of acacia trees like those you've seen growing in its habitat. Then you set a gibbon free. I had three cameras loaded and three different lenses mounted—one for when the gibbon was fairly near, another for when it was fifty feet or so away, and a huge telephoto for when it reached the treetops.

The animal I chose was a female, a gray gibbon, and the zoo director felt that she would eventually come down to him and not scamper away. The director of the zoo, Mr. Benjamin Galstaun (son of an Armenian father and an Indonesian mother), is one of the most charming, enthusiastic, and helpful persons I've ever met. He loves every one of his animals. The high point of each day I was there was the lunch prepared by his Indonesian wife, who's a superb Chinese-style cook.

I can't seem to get away from food, even for a single page. Seem to be preoccupied with good food. But, then, I'm enthusiastic about nature, art, sex, and everything else.

Back to the gibbon (which inspired me with some enthusiasm, too). At first she was afraid to climb. Judging from the expression on her face, she thought the whole thing was a nasty human trick. Then suddenly, off she went flying from branch to branch like a bird. Her long arms swung her into space, and when she couldn't reach, she flew.

She came down that night and saved *Life* the $100 I had guaranteed to pay if the zoo had to replace her. That's what a gibbon costs here; in the U.S. one would cost $1,500.

I've just been splashed—right across the face. I like it up to a point. But I wish the sea would stop pitching the *Harini* around so much. Hard to go on writing but I'll try.

Two other creatures I had not seen in the sanctuary were a leopard and a python. Leopards had left telltale fresh paw marks in the sand near the tower and near one of my camps. I'd seen the tracks, but never a leopard. I might have baited one with a pig and sat up in a tree with a flash setup, but this would hardly have gotten me a real picture in either the ethical or the aesthetic sense.

The leopard is a difficult subject. For one thing, it can move extremely fast. For another, it is very capable of killing humans. The one at the zoo was captured less than a year ago, as an adult. Foolishly, when looking for something to eat, it had climbed through a window and into an occupied hut. The people left hurriedly; once they were outside they remembered to close the exits, trapping the animal within. They knew its value.

Benjamin and I decided that the only safe place to do this leopard was in a large cage. An empty one faced south and had a little light in the afternoon. We decorated the interior of it with a small forest. Not only did we cover the cement walls with a leafy screen, but I had bushes placed throughout the cage so that I could photograph the leopard through foliage.

Though it took a lot of technical doing, the big cat was moved into the newly decorated cage without mishap. I did not realize how dear to his heart this newfound jungle would be. As soon as he was in the cage—put there through a small trapdoor— he disappeared behind the bushes. Completely disappeared. I couldn't see even one spot.

After several hours of being screamed at and prodded with long bamboo poles, he showed himself for a moment or two— and then hid someplace else. This happened again and again and as a result, it took two days for me to get the needed shots.

The python was another matter. I first planned to decorate another cage and put a squirrel and the python together. The pythons in the Djakarta zoo eats three times a month. Each meal consists of an adult chicken, which is alive. The python grabs the chicken's head with its jaws and then winds a fold of his great body around the bird, crushing it to death. Then the python slowly swallows the chicken's head first, then the body, which it pushes into its mouth from behind with one of its coils. Benjamin showed me a series of photographs showing a python eating a full-grown deer in just the same way it would eat a chicken. Hard to believe—until you realize a python's jaws unhinge when necessary, transforming its mouth into the gaping hole of a huge sack.

I had an idea for a great photograph: a shot past the body of a paralyzed-with-fear squirrel to the striking head of the snake. It was a pipe dream. The python feeds only at dusk or at night and is unpredictable about how long it will go without a decent meal. What's more, the squirrel was bound to climb up the wire screen of the cage.

I settled for letting the python out of its cage for a nice afternoon crawl. Eight men carried it to a piece of ground on which some thick bamboo clumps were growing and set it loose. Another twenty men were on hand to hem it in; some of them carried white sheets, which pythons are said be afraid of.

The first thing this beast did was slide into the thickest clump of bamboo and wind its coils around several big stalks. It then proceeded to remain inviolate and invisible for an hour. Finally, after some of the bamboo had been cut away, an old man, the snakekeeper, got his hand behind the snake's head, and some assistants unwound its body.

The second time the python was placed on the ground, I kept its attention by going as close to it as I could. It struck at me several times, but it always missed by at least a foot. I wasn't in any danger, for the python has no poison in its fangs. It can, however, administer a very nasty bite. The green snake Sohib caught near the tower last month was much more dangerous.

Getting rougher on the *Harini* now, and harder to write. However, since there's nothing much else to do . . .

I spent about five days at the zoo, taking photographs, enjoying the animals, and being with the Galstauns. I'd decided that I needed about two weeks away from Udjong Kulon; it finally came to three. Since I had done the photography for the *Time-Life* cookbook on Japan earlier this year, I knew something about the series. One of the books coming up was Southeast Asia, and this prompted me to cable Dick Williams, the cookbook editor, and Bob Mason, the picture editor of the book division, volunteering my services. They were gladly accepted, and I now could travel to Sumatra and Bali—and get paid to do it.

The *Harini* is now entering Tamandjaja Bay. Before we land, I'm going to try to photograph a "bagand" or fishing tower. I described these bamboo towers, some of which are as far as a mile from shore, previously. Their lanterns guided the *Harini* into the harbor when I returned from Djakarta last month. But then I didn't get the picture I want now: one lovely tower in the middle of the bay, the bright light of the tower's lamps reflected in the water, and two men silhouetted on the top against the darkening sky—a good subject for a photographer and a very good picture for the cookbook.

October 24, 9 P.M.

The *Harini* picked up the men in Tamandjaja en route to the sanctuary. Effendy met me at the Hotel Indonesia the morning I left. I'm in the deckhouse of the *Harini*. Made the "bagand"

228

This thirty-foot python has no poisonous fangs, but kills crushing its victims

Overleaf:
Eight men were needed at the Djakarta Zoo to cart the python to an outdoor setting.

pictures at dusk, in the very few minutes when it was still light enough to see the tower against the sky and also dark enough that the lamps dominated. It's now totally dark. The moon hasn't risen yet, and the *Harini* is being navigated by observations of the land mass of Java, on the left of the ship as it proceeds almost due west. There is no compass on the *Harini*. All navigation is strictly by observation. If it's too dark to see, the ship is stopped, and it never goes out of sight of land. This primitive, but cautious navigation isn't quite as good as that practiced on the *Tiare Taporo* (the name means "lime blossom" in Tahitian), the copra schooner on which I sailed from Papeete to the Marquesas. The *Tiare Taporo* was often out of sight of land, and the skipper, who was tipsy most of the time, navigated by ocean swell and the movement of waves, by the smell from land, and by sheer instinct—and always found his way.

I've been trying to read *Greenmantle* by John Buchan, the author of *The Thirty-nine Steps*. It's a good book, except for the author's attempt at writing American dialogue—what a mess.

The *Harini* is moving too much for me either to read or to write, and since I can't seem to catnap, I guess I'll just sit and try to think about pleasant things for the two hours we have to go.

Wednesday, October 25, 10:30 P.M.

At the table near the front window of the tower. Heard peacocks crying early this morning. Later discovered I now have a large family of chickens. The two hens that were setting when I left—the ones whose eggs I coveted but couldn't get—have produced sixteen chicks; one hen has eleven, and the other five. Not only that, but the big black goat that Enang sold me for 1,000 rupiahs was apparently pregnant when I bought her, for she can no longer conceal her condition. This means that I won't have her slaughtered for goat stew and "sate," that nice Indonesian specialty Sohib made when I had the Schenkels to dinner last month.

Some of the trees near the tower have burst into lavender blossom, with a lovely effect. I remember seeing the same kind of trees, also in bloom, lining some of the streets in Djakarta, where Effendy identified them as *Lagerstroemia speciosa*. I'd seen these trees on previous trips to Djakarta, but without the distinctive flowers, so I didn't associate them with the trees here.

At six this morning I sent the Schenkels the mail I'd picked up for them at the Swiss Embassy. Some of the letters were slightly burned in a fire in the Djakarta post office. I've been partially circumventing this post office by including my outgoing mail with my film shipments, which go Air Express to New York. Incoming mail has been very erratic.

4:45 P.M. The bantengs are now in the clearing, over to the right. Near them a big peacock is strolling. At the far end of the clearing, a single brilliant white note against the green turned out to be an egret when I looked at it through my binoculars.

I'll miss this clearing with its simple, unspoiled, and quite undramatic beauty.

4:50. Just set up a 600mm Kilfit lens. *Life* sent it in September, but it was inexplicably left in the Bangkok airport for three weeks. I found it waiting for me in Djakarta during my last visit. Don't need any more pictures of bantengs, but I can't resist seeing these animals so clearly in the warm afternoon light. The baby banteng I first saw in August is now half grown. And now there's a second young one. There are just three females today, not four. And there's a big black bull—probably the one I saw previously. My fondness for these animals, despite their pastoral appearance, was greatly diminished when I discovered that the Balinese had domesticated them. On Bali they graze peace-

...leaf:
...al view of the
...ral stupa sur-
...ded by seventy-
...smaller ones, each
...hich contains a
...size statue of
...dha.

Grotesque rainspout is
on the southwest
corner of the stupa's
fourth terrace.

The south side of the
third terrace combines
bas-relief and
sculpture-in-the-round
devoted to Buddha.

Overleaf:
Buddha in meditation
is part of a group on
the fourth terrace. The
bas-relief depicts
Buddha being tempted
by women.

fully, with wooden clapper bells—their marks of servility—hung from their necks.

5:05. Made a few shots of the young one, to compare with those I made in August, and to try out this huge cannonlike lens. Think it's better than my short but clumsy mirror lens.

5:20. Now the bantengs have run off, perhaps to prove their shyness, for two men from the *Harini* appeared. The men took the shortcut across the edge of the clearing to go to the Tjidaon for a bath. I suppose I could ask them to go the other way. But it's twice as far, and I already have the bantengs. I get tired of being an ogre.

5:45. Anda has just come from scouting the Hiur rhino wallow with Enang. As I feared, not a single fresh sign—they were looking for droppings, since there's no mud to show tracks. No reason for the rhino to go to a bone-dry wallow.

7 P.M. To come back to my coverage of Indonesia, Udjong Kulon, where I had been working for almost two months, is only a few miles away across the Sunda Strait from Sumatra, but there was no way to reach there from the sanctuary. Our boat, the *Harini,* was too small to make that kind of crossing. But there are several flights a week from Djakarta to points in Sumatra, and Tommy and I chose to go to Padang, in Western Sumatra. The major reason for determining my choice was the architecture there. Almost every building is topped by a fantastic roof. The photograph shown here demonstrates, better than words, the half arc sweep of the rooftop almost like a scimitar sitting on its lower curve, the two ends pointing up toward the sky. A perfect example of this architecture was a farmhouse at Minangkabau, with a group of ducks paddling in the pond in front of it. The land itself is also beautiful. Again like Bali, rice is the main staple and every available portion of land is used for its cultivation. Of course other foods are also cultivated, and we saw soy bean plants being beaten with sticks to separate the beans from the stalks and pods.

A subject that is almost always pictorial is the seaside, and Western Sumatra was no exception. We drove to the fishing village of Teluk Nisung and spent half a day photographing the activity. A group of men were pulling in a long net which had been set offshore and I found an interesting custom. Many of the fish here are very small and if parts of the fish bodies stick out of the mesh of the net, the children of the village are allowed to scramble over this, grabbing as many as they can while the net is still being brought in. I made one photograph of some of these children proudly exhibiting the filled small metal dishes they use to collect their catch. The most picturesque pedlar's stand I ever saw was when an old man carefully arranged several kinds of small fish he had bought from the fishermen and then put the tray on his head. It was actually a hat.

We drove northwest of Padang into the region in which coconuts are the main crop. I noticed a man walking along the road with a large monkey on a leash and I thought, "How quaint." When I saw a second man about ten miles farther on, again with a monkey, I decided we had better stop and investigate. I quickly learned that the animals were not pets, but able workers. They climb to the top of the coconut palms which are about fifty feet tall here. Guided by hand signals and jerks on the rope attached to their collars, the monkeys twist free the ripe coconuts which fall to the ground. I made some photographs of one monkey which was four years old. He had been captured when one and carefully trained by his owner. The monkey is fed coconut meat and is a willing worker.

The small fish on this man's hat is not for decoration but for sale.

*erleaf:
nkeys that harvest
coconuts in Parit
lintang are guided
tugs on the rope
d hand signals.*

The roofs of the
coconut market in
Sitjintjin are the
typical crescent shape
found in West
Sumatra.
Women prepare and
sell roast pig and
other delicacies at a
cockfight in Bali.

Overleaf:
These men are carry-
ing nets away from the
shore to the drying
racks.

Right:
Children proudly
display fish garnered
from the nets.

At Teluk Nibung in
Sumatra, children
scramble for fish
sticking out of the
nets.

On the *Harini* bound for the mouth of the Tjigenter. The men already have a line overboard, hoping to catch a large fish. They're taking their fishing a little more seriously after the fuss I made yesterday. We arrived here on Tuesday at 10:45 P.M., carrying with us the one king mackerel, or "tenggiri" (as it's called in Indonesian), caught en route. I expected the *Harini* to set its net Wednesday night. Yesterday morning, when I asked why no fish had been delivered, I was told that the net was torn and there was no nylon to repair it with. I was really furious, since the *Harini* has received enough charter money to pay for half of its original cost. Ong's excuse was that nylon was unavailable in Labuan. At this I threatened to reduce the charter fee, because the agreement included fish, and suggested he get a move on and try to troll for some large ones on the west side of Peutjang. In one hour he returned with four fish. One, a "tongkol" (this fish is the false albacore, *Euthynnus alletteratus*), weighed about five pounds. Two of the other three were barracuda, the first I've seen here; one weighed about four pounds, and the other—a monster—weighed at least thirty. The fourth fish, a long skinny one that flies above the water in long leaps but isn't a true flying fish, is called "kakatjangan" here. The local name for barracuda is "tombang," and the Latin name for the king mackerel is *Scomberomorus guttatus*. (Effendy, who lectures in biology, was kind enough to look these up when we were away from the sanctuary.) We have salted and fried half of the fish and are taking it with us to the Tjigenter. I left the other half with Enang and Sanara, who are staying behind to guard headquarters.

Sohib and Amir are on the *Harini* now, but since they spent three weeks alone at the tower, I've given them a short leave. Sohib will be dropped off in Tamandjaja, and Amir is going to Labuan. Both of them will return when the *Harini* does, hopefully the 29th. So I wouldn't be shorthanded at the Tjigenter, Dr. Schenkel was kind enough to lend me a man, Djaja, for the few days until the *Harini* returns.

There'll be a lot to do when we get to the Tjigenter this morning. First we must make a base camp. Then we'll get the canoe into the river and go upstream for about half an hour, until the water is too shallow to continue. The wallow is about a fifteen-minute walk from where we'll leave the canoe.

Effendy is to stay at the base camp. Anda, Suleman, and Djaja will come with me to build a blind overlooking the wallow. I hope to get the blind finished today. Then Anda and I will go back tomorrow morning for a two-day stay there.

My plan is to come out the second evening and to go to base camp for a bath, a walk around, etc., and then to go back at

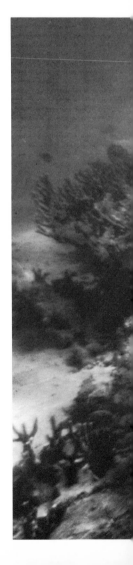

dawn the next morning. The little bit of time I have left in Udjong Kulon will allow me two stays in the blind—one on the 28th and 29th, and the other on the 30th and 31st. Possibly I'll go to it for November 1 and the morning of November 2. I must be back at the tower by nightfall November 2, and I may have to pack all night to be ready to leave Udjong Kulon, probably forever, at dawn November 3. I'm already sad at the thought of leaving. This place has come to mean a great deal to me. It will be a real wrench to go.

Underwater photograph of coral bed at Peutjang was made with a Nikonos camera fitted with a 35mm lens.

The men have just caught a "tongkol" weighing three or four pounds. This fish looks very much like those Gypsy Rose Lee catches all the time off the California coast; I hadn't noticed the similarity before. Now I remember how, a few years ago, she steamed "tongkol"-like fish in a huge kettle at her fabulous house in Beverly Hills.

Gypsy is one of the best cooks I know and an ardent fishing buff. She wrote the introduction to my first book, *Food Is a Four-letter Word,* in 1948. I read the book now with a shudder. What nerve I had to write a cookbook, knowing so little. And there's not a picture in it. It was written just to prove I could write a book, which I really cannot. Writing this diary is something else. Nowhere to go to in a blind or on a small boat, and all that energy to expel. But in New York, sitting down to a typewriter with a clean sheet of paper in it when there are so many other things one can find to do—so many reasons not to begin, or continue . . . Trying to write *The Nile,* my last book, was horrible. One of the worst experiences I ever had.

Yesterday Effendy and I went to Peutjang to have a farewell lunch with the Schenkels and their staff. The food, as usual there, was wonderful. But the great joy of the visit was a swim over the coral reef near the Peutjang shore. I had goggles but no fins, so I couldn't dive easily, but this was hardly necessary since the Peutjang shore abruptly drops off into deep water within a few feet of the beach. You can wade out to about shoulder height and then sit down on the edge of a sort of underwater cliff. Here there is an abundance of corals, some of which I had photographed during an extreme low tide that had exposed them to view. Yesterday the deep blue of the sea served as a backdrop not only for the splendidly colored and textured corals but also for a myriad of small fish.

I tried yesterday to photograph some of the fish, which are variously colored and shaped. I especially wanted the yellow fish congregating with the bright blue. But I'm no Peter Gimbel. He's America's best underwater photographer, and I thought about him several times as I floundered about yesterday. I've done several dives with a scuba outfit and weights, but they're easy compared with "goggling" as the Schenkels call it. The Schenkels love to "goggle," and their enthusiasm made me try it again despite my unpleasant memories of how, when I'd tried it before, I'd wrenched my back avoiding some sharp coral.

I've loaned the Schenkels my underwater camera for the next few days—they are so crazy about it. The large carton I brought them from Djakarta turned out to contain much-needed medicines from Switzerland. It was only eight months en route. The Schenkels leave December 1, to go back to Basle. I asked Mrs. Schenkel about the food she had promised to pick up for Amir and Sohib. One of her staff had been instructed to take care of it and he forgot.

Saturday, October 28, 2:15 P.M.

Not very happy about our situation here. We've built a tree house, but not over a rhino wallow.

Lack of communication is always a problem in a foreign country, especially in the Orient, where not only the language but also the culture is so different from our own. It's that way here. What was described to Anda and then me as a rhino wallow turned out to be only an upstream bank of the river. In about a mile we found five different rhino trails leading from the forest to the riverbank. Choosing which slot to work over was like playing rhino roulette. Which path would the rhino take to go for a drink of water or a bath? Anyone's guess was as good as mine.

It took Anda, Suleman, and Djaja—with a little help from Effendy and even less from me—eight hours to build the new blind, at a slot chosen almost at random. We started yesterday afternoon and completed it this morning. The men have all gone upriver another ten minutes' paddle to bathe where the water is sweet before Suleman, Djaja, and Effendy return to the camp near the shore. Anda will stay with me.

The only foreign tool used was my folding Swedish saw. Some Indonesian rope to fasten the light tree trunks used as the primary support was utilized to save time, which is running out. I contributed a waterproof nylon tarp for the roof. Everything else is made of branches and palm fronds and held together with stripped rattan runners.

Right now I'm fairly comfortable in the blind. Anda should be back soon, and he and I will stay up here until dusk tomorrow, when we'll go back to base camp. We'll come back to the blind Monday at dawn and stay until noon Wednesday, November 1. At that point it's all over. Wednesday afternoon, back to the tower to pack. I'll leave about 2 A.M. Thursday so I can arrive at Tamandjaja at dawn, drop the men, and reach Labuan at about 2 P.M. Thursday. Kumar, the driver, will be waiting there.

I won't take anything but my cameras off the *Harini* in Labuan, since the tide isn't high until 8 P.M., and I do not care to unload heavy camping gear in the surf. Effendy will stay in Labuan, supervise the unloading of the equipment, have it loaded into a small truck, and then follow me to Djakarta. He'll arrive sometime Friday morning, and I'll then have two days, Friday and Saturday, November 3 and 4, to pack my personal luggage and cameras that are going with me, pack the rest of the photo equipment and send it air freight (but on the same plane with me by arrangement with Japan Air Lines), and pack the camping gear and send it sea freight. I leave at 10 A.M. on Sunday, November 5, for Tokyo; I'll spend two days there and be in New York on the 8th.

2:30 P.M. I've discovered the company I'll have near the blind. Just a minute ago a brilliant stork-billed kingfisher

stopped on a large dead log in the middle of the river below. I'm about twenty feet above the water; the tree house is about fifteen feet above the ground, and the ground's about five feet above the river. Yesterday a large kingfisher followed us along the river. At the end he became so used to us that we were able to bring the canoe within fifteen feet of him. Needless to say, I made some pictures of him. He kept turning, and cocking his head as if to ask, And who are you? I got several shots of him in this pose. Later he missed a fish right in front of us, looked very mad, and settled on a log near the water, to stay there for quite a while before he got up again and tried for another fish.

2:35. The men have been gone almost an hour, and I'm furious. The longer they wait to come back the longer it will be for this area to settle down. I should never have allowed them to go, but I thought Effendy had more sense than to linger. My

A stork-billed king-fisher followed our canoe up the river and kept cocking his head at us.

e rope in our canoe
hich Anda is
dling) was used
onstructing the
e house overlook-
the Tjigenter.

259

chances of getting a rhino are so slim anyway.

What I have here is a well-used rhino ditch leading from the bank to the river. The rhinos apparently go into the water, which is shallow, have a bit of a bath, and exit at another ditch, farther up the river. The blind is on the north side of the river, so a rhino won't be able to smell it, and even though rhinos can't see very well, it's considerably above their usual line of vision. A rhino will, I hope, enter the river about seventy feet from the blind.

There is very little light except at high noon, when the sun is just between the high trees that line the banks. With Koda-chrome, most of the day it will be about 1/30 second at F2.8 or F4. Luckily I'll be close enough to work with the 105mm lens, resting it on the railing I have in front of me at the right height for it. I also have high-speed Ektachrome to use when

Anda kept close watch from our tree house blind on the Tjigenter while the author wrote in his diary.

necessary, but I'd prefer not to use it; it has more grain than the Kodachrome and no snap.

It's 2:45 and the men are back. Suleman, Djaja, and Effendy are about ready to leave. Before they push off I'll have Effendy take a couple of shots of me in the tree house from the canoe. The pictures will be nice to have.

4:45. I'm restless, and have been for the last two hours. Not too much, but I've tried all my lenses and checked the changing light every half hour. If something appears I want to be ready. I have three Nikons sitting near me.

Part of the author's team: standing left to right, Sanara, Anda, and Enang; seated, Sohib and Suleman.

The blind is small and triangular. Finding three trees near enough to each other to support a platform—and within view of a rhino trail—wasn't easy. It's not too crowded though.

I've already blown up my air mattress and inserted it in my sleeping bag. I sleep on top of this quite comfortably; even use

a white sheet. At about three in the morning it gets cool enough to pull another sheet over you.

It's cooling somewhat now. Was about 100 degrees in the shade at noon. At the zoo last week it was 95°F. on an open veranda at 2 P.M. Because of the heat, I'm down to wearing a pair of white boxer shorts—and nothing else.

A pandanus mat is alongside the sleeping bag. Anda will sleep on the mat.

At the short end of the triangular blind is a split-bamboo box with my supplies. The larger Nikon case is next to my head. Also next to my head are the three small teddy bears in three sizes, Papa and the two little girls, given to me by Elin and Jill years ago; I must take them with me on all my trips. Bringing them to the tree house is carrying this very far, but it's as close as I can come to bringing the girls themselves. Someday I'll take them on an interesting assignment, not just sight-seeing in Europe.

Everything else I've with me in the blind—including my knapsack with spare clothing and my war bag with its first-aid kit, insect repellent, bug bomb, toilet paper, flashlight, etc.— is hanging on the low walls. My tiny kerosene Primus stove is outside, and tomorrow at about 5 A.M., before any sensible animal should think of coming here, I'll go below and make coffee. I also have eggs to cook, spaghetti, corned beef hash, and chili with beans. Brought a pail of cooked rice from camp. And of course, have, as I always do, a supply of tomato herring. Then too, there are as usual, extras.

For lunch today I had Beluga caviar, not very salted which my best girl gave me when I left New York. With it went chopped onion and egg on pumpernickel and a salad of avocado, tomato, and cucumber with my own salad dressing. For dessert, a really good mango. For tomorrow, the box still contains a few goodies, including a small can of Brie. I had Chablis with the caviar today, tomorrow I'll have Almaden Mountain Red Burgundy with the cheese.

5:45. Have been reading Han Suyin's *The Mountain Is Young*. A sensitive book, fiction, on Nepal. Makes me want to go there. I also have and am part way into Robert Graves's *Wife to Mr. Milton* and Thomas Wolfe's *You Can't Go Home Again*. All three of these books are from the unofficial lending library of the American Embassy in Djakarta, where I was given borrowing privileges. I intend to leave all my own paperbacks there, just as interest.

While sitting here I've been thinking of how lucky I am to do what I want to, not just on weekends but day in and day out, to go everywhere in the world and savor it. Money alone could never have given me the privileges I've enjoyed: experiencing strange landscapes, primitive peoples, exotic arts. For thirty years my camera has been a magic carpet.

5:55. Now that it's approaching sundown all the small noises of the forest—the sounds of insects rubbing their legs together, voices of birds, the creakings of branches rubbing each other— are getting louder. All these sounds are heard against a backdrop of palm fronds that rises in serried layers from the river finally to outline the narrow corridor of sky above. There are a few disturbing insects—midges, which are small flies that bite, and ants—but not too many mosquitoes; nevertheless, I take my antimalaria pills like some people do religion—fervently.

Sunday, October 29, exactly 5:30 A.M.

Anda and I have finished our breakfast. Coffee (real coffee— pot boiled) and bread (from Djakarta) with butter and apricot jam. Two slices each. Have washed the dishes, lifted my mosquito net out of the way, folded and put away the bed sheet. Now we're ready for business.

Read a chapter of *The Mountain Is Young* last night. Reading by kerosene lamp is difficult, but the book got me out of my environment, and about 7:30 P.M., put me to sleep. Was awakened at 3:30 by an unholy racket below. Anda would have slept through it if I hadn't roused him.

Turned out to be nothing more than a large bird working the river—and making enough racket for a large animal.

It's going to be a long and hot day. I am wearing a small blue towel around my middle, fastened with a safety pin. This is much cooler than shorts, since the air can get under it. Because I perspired very much yesterday, I took a salt tablet this morning. I do not want the depressed feeling you get from salt exhaustion.

Made our coffee this morning on the tiny Primus stove I took up the Ruwenzori with me in 1959. It made "porridgi," as the Africans call oatmeal, near the Margherita Glacier at above 15,000 feet. Took forever, since high altitude slows cooking down enormously. We're very much at sea level here.

Also made a pot of tea this morning and filled my pint thermos and one of the canteens. I like having a canteen of cold tea. It tastes better than boiled water, which I don't have to drink on this trip because I brought along two five-gallon cans of the Hotel Indonesia's water. I took them from Djakarta, thinking I was going to be camping in the dry area of the Hiur wallow. Now we're on a river and have sweet water upstream from us, especially at low tide, since the ocean water comes up and goes down the river with the tides. But it's good to have filtered water, and coffee made with it tastes much, much better than boiled-river-water coffee. Last night I was thinking of the extraordinary distances food—especially Eliot Elisofon's—travels today. My meals yesterday were an example. Breakfast was Quaker Oats made in Australia and cooked with powdered milk from the U.S., coffee from the U.S., and a local tangerine. Lunch included Beluga caviar (it originally came from Russia, but it was purchased and given to me in New York), salad with dressing made from (among other things, Italian olive oil and California cider vinegar), pumpernickel from Holland, and an onion, an egg, and also fresh fruit from Djakarta. For dinner I had a slice from each of two salamis, one from Italy and the other from New York, then half a small can of French Brie on Dutch pumpernickel and another slice of Dutch pumpernickel with American peanut butter and Australian apricot jam. I still have part of the tiny jar of raspberry jam my daughter Elin bought at the July Fourth fair in Vinalhaven. I can't seem to bring myself to use it up. Before going to bed, I had two tiny squares of Dutch chocolate. There was also the French Chablis and California Almaden Mountain Red Burgundy.

Can't seem to get started writing about my food trip through Indonesia. Perhaps it would be better to generalize at first. Writing in longhand is difficult—so much to say, and the words come too quickly for the hand to keep up with them. It's 6 A.M. now; took me a half hour to write the preceding.

Indonesian food is not the greatest. Sorry to start with a negative statement, but that's what comes to mind. If I hadn't had several meals in people's homes, particularly the one cooked at the Schenkels' house by Djuhari and Widodo, I'd have had a very poor impression indeed. The Indonesian dishes cooked at the Inter-Continental hotels (the Indonesia and Bali Beach) aren't very good, for they're altered to fit so-called international taste. I must say, however, that the two hotels are extremely well managed. To digress for a moment, because it is interesting and comes to mind, the first meal I had at the Hotel Indonesia on my last trip to Djakarta was European, so European as to be ridiculous—headcheese vinaigrette and blanquette of veal on noodles. My taste had become so accustomed to the spicy style of Indonesia that I could hardly eat it.

Spiciness is the chief characteristic of Indonesian food. Indonesian cooks use many more spices, and in greater quantities, than do cooks anywhere else I've ever been. And the resultant dishes are usually hot. We don't have separate words for hot in temperature and hot in taste; the Indonesians do. I must say here that their food is often hot in taste and unfortunately cold in temperature. Indonesians think nothing of preparing a dinner, even for company, hours in advance; they'll set out at least a half-dozen platters around a tureen of rice and then eat it cold. Some of their dishes are prepared with coconut oil, and its effect cold leaves something to be desired. The hot taste comes from two kinds of chili peppers—long, skinny green ones, which are moderate, and small red ones, which are murder. I made a very hot sauce at the camp by slicing a few of the small ones and covering them with gin in a small bottle. I once saw this done by Indian waiters in Suva, Fiji.

6:15 A.M. Anda just climbed down and brought up his white rice, some peanuts, and a piece of the "tongkol" the *Harini* men caught Thursday. Often the people here salt their fish thoroughly and then fry it hard. Fish treated like this keeps for several days, even at 100-degree temperatures.

Peanuts provide one of the most important Indonesian flavors. Sometimes they're ground and mixed with hot pepper to make a sauce called "tamal," which is added (to individual taste) to almost any dish. Fried peanuts are used as a protein on rice, as are bits of salted fish. The poor man's diet here is rice with peanuts, cooked small beans (there are several varieties of these), thin noodles, and salted fish. In Tamandjaja and elsewhere the people catch many tiny fish, salt them, and then dry them whole on racks or mats in the sun. One day suffices to dehydrate the fish, which can then be kept for a month. The tiny fish are usually fried in coconut oil and eaten with rice. Larger fish are treated and used the same way, but are much more costly.

6:30. Just stopped to make a few quick shots of Anda eating his rice with fish and peanuts. He's eating with his right hand, without a fork, from a tin plate. Indonesians often eat from banana leaves. Forks and spoons are rarely used in the countryside.

To come back to spices. The next predominant taste is that of coconut oil, the cooking fat of Indonesia. True, you can buy canned margarine, but this is a foreign introduction. I use it because I got tired of every fish, chicken, and vegetable tasting of coconut oil, which does not have the tasteless virtue of peanut oil and the various vegetable oils made in the U.S. Sometimes it does add an agreeable flavor. I particularly like it for deep-fried squid.

The Moluccas, which most people know as the famous Spice Islands, are in eastern Indonesia, near West Irian. From them cloves, nutmegs, mace, peppercorns, and other spices are exported to the whole world. Indonesians use all of these spices. In addition, they use three roots, all of which look like ginger in structure; one is bright yellow and is probably turmeric. They also use a paste made from tamarinds. Salt, which is obtained from sea water, is sold in block form.

Some Indonesian dishes are made with a cream obtained by grating and then pressing coconut meat. This cream is made

and used in all the central and south Pacific islands. During my voyage on the *Varua* I stopped on an atoll in the Solomons and there had fresh fish cooked in coconut cream with salt and red peppers. During another stopover on that same voyage I had the best fried fish of my life: grouper dipped in batter and deep fried in peanut oil from Hong Kong. It had been killed with a stick of dynamite by my Australian host (he and his wife owned a copra plantation on a Solomon Island outlier). While I'm remembering, there was also a big bunch of Torres Strait pigeons (these have green wings and are larger than U.S. pigeons) he shot and I cooked. After marinating the breasts in soy sauce, bourbon, sugar, garlic, and ginger, I broiled them on coconut rinds; the other parts of the pigeons went into a soup.

My food trip covered Java, Bali, and Sumatra, three of the largest islands in a chain of hundreds, and enough territory for my purposes. Sumatra's food is distinguished by being too hot for most Javanese. In Djakarta several restaurants feature Sumatran cooking. I went to one with Amir Daud, who is from Sumatra. He was amazed at the way I could take the hot food, but, then, he hasn't been to Mexico or Peru. One pepper used in Lima is so hot that the locals call it the Spanish equivalent of son of a bitch. None of this means that I enjoy food in which you can taste only fire. This food is just as bad as, or worse than, some French food in which whatever was there originally has long since departed and you can taste only the sauce. I must say I prefer cooking where the good taste of meat or fish is still there. And I am not a meat-and-potatoes man—not by a long shot. But right now I would like a charcoal-broiled steak and a foil-wrapped potato baked in the embers. I'll be in New York in just ten days, and this will be one of my first meals. There's practically no decent beef in Indonesia. All the beef here is sold fresh and is very tough. Some water buffalo meat is used. This tastes very much like ordinary beef, especially so since it is always prepared with spicy sauces. The best "sate" I had was in Pedang, West Sumatra; it was made from sea turtle.

Although curry is very Indian, most of the meat, fish, and chicken dishes in Indonesia are curries of one sort of another. At least, they're called curries. Curry isn't a single spice, as some people think it is, rather, it's a combination of many spices and varies from one part of India to another. Indonesian curry is different from Indian curry and also varies. All Indonesian food here is eaten with rice that has been washed, put into a pot with salt and water, and cooked over a fire until the water's gone. The size of the fire is important. You start rice with a hot fire and as water diminishes you must also lower the heat so as not to burn the rice. The rice comes out not quite in flaky indi-

da, like most
donesians, eats a
ical meal with his
gers: rice, fried fish,
d peanuts.

267

vidual grains, but also not quite in a gooey mess. That at the bottom of the pot is usually caked together, which doesn't mean it's not eaten. Rice is made once a day, and it's served cold, even with warm food. It's usually kept in a square basket woven from split bamboo. One of the classic Indonesian dishes is "nasi goreng," fried rice. The cold rice is fried in coconut oil with bits of shrimp, chicken, or whatever is available, as well as onion, and an omelet is sliced over it when it's finished.

I left garlic and onion out of my list of spices, which was a mistake, since both are used. Fried sliced onions are used as a topping for soups (like Chinese broth), for noodles, and for several other dishes. The quick snack in Indonesia (and also in Thailand, where I tasted it earlier this year) is noodles cooked in a meat or gizzard broth with a few vegetables and then topped with chopped green onions or fried regular ones. The most-used onion here is a small red one about the size of a shallot.

Fried crackers often accompany meals. The best of the crackers are the pink ones made with pulverized dry shrimp and cassava. Tapioca (another name for cassava) is used as a flour; so is rice. Wheat flour is rarely used.

Indonesia is a rice nation, with two types of rice: that grown in irrigated plots, and that grown in dry upland ones. To speak of irrigated rice paddies is to speak of Bali, for nowhere else in the world is there the magnificence seen in Bali's beautifully terraced hillsides and in the water moving down them. Bali produces two crops of rice each year. Unlike Java and Sumatra, which depend upon rain, Bali has ample water from spring-fed rivers, which give it an emerald-green aspect throughout the year. The contrast between Bali's fertile fields and the dry brown fields of western Java was something I found visually shocking.

It's only 8 A.M. This is going to be a long day. I stopped writing a few minutes ago because Anda spotted a large monitor lizard crawling under the bamboo some yards from the blind. I was somewhat surprised, because the wind is between us. The blind is almost due west of the rhino path on the other side of the river, which is about twelve yards wide. I'd have preferred to be completely downwind, due north, but on that part of the bank there were no trees near enough to the rhino path to build a house in.

I'm going to read for a while, and Anda will keep watch. We'll both hear a rhino—if one ever comes.

9:50. Just had my breakfast—or, rather, snack, since I had coffee, bread, butter, and jam at about five. Finished the small jar of caviar.

My eating activated Anda, who already had had his rice, peanuts, and fish, to eat again. Not much else to do fifteen feet above the ground and in a triangular space only about ten feet long and five and a half feet wide at its widest end.

A strong wind just came by, and was very welcome. I'm writing while sitting down on my air mattress. My desk is a ten-inch-high Halliburton camera case. It's good enough.

Thinking of going to Thomas Wolfe now. Han Suyin overwrites and overdescribes, albeit beautifully.

10:30. Read about fifty pages of Wolfe. Some years ago I worked with Paul Baker at Baylor University in Waco, Texas, on a theater production *Of Time and the River*. I was involved in doing the lighting, all of which was in color, and in the production of film for projection on scrims hung in front of the stage. Behind the scrims dramatic action took place while the film was being shown. This was one of the first of the new multimedia experiments. At one point a group of actors—all dressed alike, like a Greek chorus—stood between two scrims and were covered with film images from three projectors while they recited a Wolfe poem. All the images were different. One, of a white wisteria vine in bloom, was spread with an amorphic lens to a width of about fifty feet. Two other, smaller images, of pink and red blossoms, were bombarded onto the white one. They produced countless different montages as the projectors swung from side to side. The second scrim was twenty feet farther away, making for a larger image and for depth.

Ray Bradbury has written a space drama, *Leviathan 99*, which I'm hoping to direct at Baker's new theater in San Antonio. A far cry—all of this—from Udjong Kulon, and also from Indonesian food, to which I must come back, at least as a vehicle to discuss the country.

It may seem to be obvious, too much so, but it was Bali which really captured me. In spite of its renown and the book *Island of Bali* written by my very good friend, now gone, Miguel Covarrubias, and in spite of all the claims I'd heard about Bali, I went there as a doubter.

True, all the young girls now wear ghastly pink or yellow brassieres with at least four inches of fabric below the cups and with laces at the back like those on old-fashioned corsets, while all the old women shamelessly bare their breasts—to their waists. But the beauty of Bali—Bali is the finest example of man-made nature I've ever seen—

We admire wild, unspoiled landscapes, like those of the Grand Tetons or the island of Mooréa off Tahiti, but in Bali almost everything has been reshaped by man's hand. The result hasn't been the usual disaster of mines and factories, tenements and assorted architectural eyesores. Rather, it's been rice terraces built in long curving masses, on every part of this island. The water starts at the top of the hill and works its stepped way

The Balinese construct
life-size scarecrows to
frighten away the
birds from the ripen-
ing rice.

A man and his wife
have just finished
planting young rice in
a flooded paddy.

Overleaf:
A Balinese family
pounds newly har-
vested rice in wood
mortars to remove
husks from the grai

to the lowest terrace. Why is this so beautiful? I've thought a lot about it. I believe that it is the perfect sense of order and also the sense of plenty, of the productivity of the land, which appeals to us. There is repetition, but within it there is variation of line and mass. And there is fresh green. What a lovely color a rice paddy is! When the sun is low enough to back-light each blade of the plants there's a yellow-green glow, rich and jewel-like—and it covers whole landscapes. When you're driving in Bali, all this is relieved at every tiny village by a small Hindu temple, each temple seemingly more ornate than the last. Carved in stone, the temples are weathered with mosses and lichens, yet nothing can obscure their enormous embellishment and detail. Here is Hindu art at its maximum charge. I cannot call it splendor, for the temples are almost garish. Luckily, they have not been painted, as have some contemporary Indian ones.

Bali's oldest temples date back to the Hindu period, as early as the seventh century. Bali alone in Indonesia has remained Hindu. Each temple has an ornate gate and a pair of entrance guardians, usually Laki and Laka, the god and goddess of death. Some of the newer temples have lions, or even mermaids. I photographed both old temples and new, finding the differences interesting. Speaking of differences, one of the reasons why Bali made such an impression on me was that my visit to it came after two months in a primeval jungle.

3:00 P.M. Very cloudy now. Almost dark on the river. And not an animal, except for one monitor lizard, all day. A fish below us—this was about an hour ago—looked like a two-foot carp.

We'll go out at five and come back early tomorrow, perhaps to stay two and a half days—if I can stand it.

Have been down only once since this morning, to relieve myself in a little pit I dug. After I used it I covered it with earth to hide the smell. I must say this is the worst vigil. Not even any notable birds to be seen all day. Some small black and yellow ones look like weavers, but I haven't seen any hanging nests.

Monday, October 30, 7:30 A.M.

Anda and I are back in the blind. We had an uneventful paddle back to shore camp yesterday; left here about 5 P.M. My watch had stopped because I couldn't bear to wear it—the wristband was so sweaty. So we left when it got too dark to take color photographs. Anyway, I don't expect a rhino to bathe except when the sun is high and it's hot.

I may be wrong, but our vigil is during the entire photographic day. Schenkel says the rhino is also nocturnal, but to do a strobe illumination of this river site would take more equipment than I have, and the result would be unpictorial. Not that

I wouldn't settle for any picture of a Java rhino at this point.

As might be expected, it rained for several hours last night. The small rains have begun. I'm sure it will pour either the day I depart or the day after that. You can't win them all.

Stayed in blind almost until dark, so dinner was late last night. The men had killed two roosters we brought here from the tower. We still have one hen here, and there are another two hens back at the tower. The roosters for yesterday's dinner were killed at noon, cleaned, and hung to cool; I particularly wanted to have a good meal last night. I cooked them with leeks, celery root, and plenty of carrots and ate two full bowls with cold boiled rice in the bottom of each. It made a fine meal. It wasn't New York chicken in the pot—no parsley or parsnips—but it was good enough.

We also had an unexpected delicacy: oysters. Oysters are found in brackish water here, just as they are in the southern U.S. When Anda and I were about five minutes from the beach, I noticed something attached to a dead log that emerged from the water with the ebbing tide. The log turned out to be covered with oysters, some of which Anda pried off with his machete. The few we managed to open on the spot were sweet and delicious, similar to some I had in the Solomons once and not unlike those sold in New Orleans. The rest we steamed open later, and they lost something in the process.

Anda goofed this morning. We had two adequate portions of chicken left for our lunch today, but he forgot to bring them along to the blind.

Effendy is coming upstream around 5 P.M., which is late enough to avoid interrupting possible photography. He's to let me know if the *Harini,* due yesterday evening, arrived today. He's also to bring me any cables and letters Amir Daud may have sent to the *Harini* to be delivered here. Effendy will also have spoken to the Schenkels, who are stopping at the Tjigenter on their way to Labuan and then to Bogor. They agreed that if by some miracle they got a shot of a rhino, they'd give the film to Amir Daud to air express to New York. They'd be given space rates and credit. I hope they got it. Schenkel borrowed a leaf from my book and built a tree house too, on a river on the western end, near the lighthouse anchorage and overlooking a rhino trail. We're both grasping at straws. But Schenkel will be here until the end of November and still has a good chance to track rhinos on wet ground.

Anda and I came back here on a really high tide. The water was up several feet on the banks. I'm watching for the turn of the tide to see if there's any tidal bore at all here. Being in a dugout canoe very similar to the ones Michael Rockefeller used on his ill-fated adventure in West Irian in 1961 (West Irian was still Dutch New Guinea at that time) made me think about him this morning. Perhaps this would be the right place to tell what I know about all this. Everyone still asks about it, and I've found that in Djakarta even the Americans think he was eaten by the natives.

Mike was a member of a Harvard expedition to Dutch New Guinea that included Karl Heider, a Harvard anthropologist working for his Ph.D., Peter Mathiessen, the author (who wrote a book, *Under the Mountain Wall,* about the area), and Robert Gardner, the expedition leader, who made a prize-winning film, *Dead Birds,* out of this study. I was along for a short period, as was Sam Putnam, a medical student and a close friend of Mike. Jan Broekhuyse, a Dutch anthropologist-administrator, was the government representative on the expedition and spoke the native language. There's no need to go into the work of the expedition in detail, for details can be found in the film, Mathiessen's book, Heider's thesis, and *Life*; Gardner is completing a book, too. Briefly, we were studying a Stone Age group that lived in the Baliem valley between two high mountain ranges and practiced a kind of formal ritual warfare with its neighbors. Mike was doing the sound for the film, and when I wasn't there he was also doing still photography with a pair of Nikons. He worked harder than any of us. Perhaps he had more to prove.

When the expedition was over, I helped convince Mike to stay on and go to the Asmat, on the southern coast, toward the west, where the people still do fantastic wood carvings. Some of these carvings—in particular totem poles twenty to thirty feet high—Mike was to collect. To help him do it the Dutch government assigned a young anthropologist from Rotterdam, René Wassing, who had practically no jungle experience.

They took two dugout canoes, very similar to the one Anda and I were in this morning and also about thirty feet long, and built a platform across their middles, separating the two hulls by about ten feet. This made a sort of a catamaran out of the two canoes. Then they built a small hut on top of the platform, modeling this affair after a similar construction made by a patrol officer in the area. The patrol officer's hut had a thatched roof; our two men used tin.

Mike had two Johnson 18-horsepower outboard motors, but at the time of the accident, only one was mounted on a canoe. To go from one village to another in the Asmat it's necessary to descend a river (all the villages are on rivers well up from the coast) and go along the coast to the river on which the next village is built. Mike and René and two natives were going up the Eilanden, the biggest river in the Asmat, when a large tidal bore, a wave of water coming back to sea (I've seen the one in the Bay of Fundy which is six feet high), swamped their canoes. The outboard submerged and ceased functioning, and the tide began to carry the catamaran out to sea. The two natives immediately jumped off and swam to shore.

8:25 A.M. A barking deer has come near the blind. Can't see him, but he is really barking. I'm almost tempted to leave the blind and try to approach him. But the rhino is my target, and I'd die if I missed my one chance by digressing. Also, the deer is on the same side of the river as the blind is, and he's downwind from it. Anda thinks he is about a hundred and fifty yards away. I obtained this opinion by asking, "Dekat?"—which means near. Anda answered "Seratus," which means a hundred, and then, "Tamba," meaning more. Very primitive communication we have.

To continue the story. René couldn't swim. There were no life preservers, although Mike, who was a superb swimmer (just for fun he swam across freezing-cold Crockett Cove every morning when the expedition was trying out its gear there before leaving for New Guinea) hardly needed one. The paddles had been swept away, and the two men tried to wrench off pieces of the tin roof to use instead. This overturned the catamaran, and Mike and René were left sitting on the two hull bottoms above the water. The tide and an offshore wind were taking them steadily out to sea. When they were out about five miles (no one will ever really know how far out they were, for though René was saved, he was almost incoherent when asked), Mike decided their situation was hopeless. The next land was Australia, hundreds of miles away in the direction in which they were drifting. He fashioned a support by connecting the gas tank from the Johnson with a five-gallon can, using his belt to connect them. Then he swam back toward the Eilanden estuary—never to be seen again.

By a miracle the two natives found a Dutch patrol officer the same day, and he radioed to Hollandia, the capital of Dutch New Guinea, and a flying boat was dispatched. The next morning, René and the canoes were found.

When the news that Mike was missing arrived in the U.S., Joan and I were giving a cocktail party at our apartment. Hugh Moffat, then the news editor of *Life,* called me and said there had been a radio flash that Mike was missing. I pooh-poohed the idea and went back to the party.

An hour later Bob Gardner called and said it was true, Mike was missing. At this point I excused myself from the party, went into another room, and packed tropical gear into a bag. I knew what was coming.

Then Moffat called again. Would I go with Governor Rockefeller to the Asmat to look for his son? I said I would if I didn't have to wear a camera around my neck. What I meant was that I would go as a friend and try to take pictures without offending anyone, including myself. Moffat agreed, and I left the party, went to the office, selected a few cameras, and joined Gardner, who was also going, at the airport.

With Governor Rockefeller came Mike's twin sister, Mary, who was almost in a state of shock, the Governor's press secretary, and a state police lieutenant, his bodyguard. We used commercial airlines to Hawaii, where we stopped for the night. I started scrounging gear: antimalaria pills, Miltowns for Mary, mosquito netting, insect repellent—things I didn't have adequate supplies of in New York and couldn't buy at night. I also bought large torches and spare batteries.

We took a charter flight to Hollandia and found that Mike was still missing—very much so, for René had been found, and we now knew the story of the disaster. We flew on to Merauke, which became search headquarters. Two small airplanes belonging to religious missions were pressed into service. A PBY, the old *Catalana* Flying Boat, arrived, and I joined its crew standing watch in a waist blister as we flew segments searching the shore for Mike. Finally the Australians flew in a huge Hercules transport plane carrying two helicopters in its belly.

We found only the gas tank along the shore, about fifteen miles east of where Mike had left the canoes. I've often thought that if the tank reached there, perhaps the raft would have as well. My opinion is that Mike never made shore. We saw so many sharks when we flew the segments, that I don't see how anyone could have survived the swim. If the sharks missed him, the swamps that line the shore are full of huge crocodiles. To say that the natives ate him is ridiculous. The people there hunt heads, or used to, but they're not cannibals. The newspapers, as usual, printed almost anything they heard from anyone, especially the Australian pressmen who came in their own airplane.

Governor Rockefeller, who had just gone through a bout of adverse publicity because of his divorce, and who had presidential aspirations, was worried that the stories of his search for Mike would look like a tearjerker attempt for sympathy. He asked the press to avoid photographing him, although this was not entirely possible. He and Mary were fair game every time they came out of the administrator's house they were living in.

I missed an extremely poignant picture of them on the first day of the search because I'd promised not to photograph them. We were on the chartered DC-3 for a long flight from Merauke to see the coast area where Mike was lost. The Australian and New Zealand pressmen, who had already arrived, joined me and writer Richard Stolley of *Life,* who came from Los Angeles. Everyone promised there'd be no pictures inside the plane. Most of those on board had had no sleep. But I'd catnapped, so when the Governor's press secretary and bodyguard couldn't keep their eyes open any longer, I was asked to watch that no pictures were taken.

We were bound back to Merauke, and the Governor and his daughter were seated together just aft of the passenger door, giving them some room in front. While I was watching, they both fell asleep. There were binoculars on the Governor's chest, and he and Mary were holding hands. It was a pathetic picture, with just enough light from the oval plane window to create an effect. How I wanted to take that picture! But I didn't.

Before the Governor and Mary awoke, two alert Australians tried to push their way past me to take the picture, and I stopped them. They couldn't believe I hadn't, and were very nasty. One of them said, "We'll see it in *Life*." But they didn't.

A book with pictures and descriptions of Mike's collection, with the pictures he made in the Asmat and with photographs I made of the sculptures, will be published in 1968 by the Museum of Primitive Art.

October 30, 10:50 A.M.

Have finished reading *The Mountain Is Young,* and Anda and I have had lunch. We finished a can of tomato herring with pumpernickel, the last avocado, and a cucumber; there was just enough dressing left. We hung the food overnight in a plastic bag sealed against ants, which have discovered our house has edibles and are very much with us now.

I've just measured the light. The sun is coloring the river, which is dotted with fallen leaves, a dull ocher. I feel like a doctor taking the temperature of a very sick patient every hour.

We ate in almost total silence, communicating by expression of face and hands. This time of day is crucial, I feel; even a rhino would want a bath in this heat.

It's really hot. Just eating is enough activity to bring out a sweat. A great advantage of the tower is how it catches wind coming across the cleared area; sometimes I thought there was too much wind, but I'd be grateful for any or all of it now.

A white flower from one of the trees hanging over the river just floated by with the tide, which is going out. I noticed the flower on these trees earlier this morning. It's pure white, with five crinkled petals. The size and texture are about the same as are found in the large iris; but the whole flower—petals and all (there doesn't seem to be any sepals)—is one continuous struc-ture: a tube about four inches long flaring into the flower and bearing stamens fastened to its inside near the top.

Thinking about Bali again. Covarrubias mentioned in his book how horrible the dogs were there. The island teems with them. They are the scavengers, even of children's feces. And there are thousands and thousands of them. And they bark incessantly at every stranger. I should have made some close-ups of these curs. I finally became very adept at hitting them with small stones, and I love animals.

The Balinese, being Hindu, will not destroy any of them. This did not prevent them from slaughtering fifty thousand human beings after the abortive Communist coup in 1965. This seems hard to believe today. They are so sweet and friendly. Too friendly sometimes for a photographer. Every time they see a camera, they all run into the scene, gaping and grinning at the lens. In America we call people like this lens lice. They're all over Indonesia. They cry, "Portret! Portret!"—which means photograph—in case other bystanders might miss being in the picture, and if you're sneaking up on a group, hoping against hope to get a shot or two before you're seen, someone going by on a bicycle will cry, "Portret! Portret!" The words are like a death knell.

Three hundred thousand men and women were killed in Indonesia in 1965. They were Communists, members of the PKI. This mass slaughter was both an act of revenge and an act of extermination. In that year, the PKI, the official Communist party in Indonesia, which numbered three million and was aided and abetted by Chinese Communists in Djakarta, attempted a coup against Sukarno's government. Some think Sukarno was in on it, but this has never been established.

The coup started and stopped in less than one day. Some army units directed by Communist officers and party men abducted six of the country's leading generals, part of the governing group of twelve, called the Council of the Generals. They tried for all twelve, but some were away from their homes, and several were too well guarded. One who got away is the present acting president, General Suharto. It was he who led the crack troops that immediately smashed the rebellion.

The six generals died hideously. They were brought to a spot called the Place of the Crocodiles. All of them were mutilated by women who cut their male organs to pieces with razor blades; arms and legs were lopped off; and all the remains were thrown into a deep well. During this procedure, a large group of women performed weird pagan dances around the scene. All of this is part of the official record made during the investigation that followed.

It can be understood that the army had a grievance and did nothing at first to stop the vengeance that came as the aftermath of the generals' deaths. But not that three hundred thousand men and women were rounded up, brought to open graves, often dug on sandy beaches, where the digging was easier, and beheaded with long swords while still standing. Many of the important members of the PKI got away and are still looked for today.

12:40 P.M. This is what is known as luck. It's raining. Some thunder, and now light rain.

Three days of real rain, and I could have gone to my rhino wallow. Now, and here, it is not only of no use, but a nuisance. It's probably not going to rain enough to do much more than offer me a last taunt.

Anyway, I'm now glad I had the nylon tarp put up. It's a bit too short to roof the whole blind. So our cell is now even smaller than it was before. I thought of it as a cell earlier today, when I went down for a moment to spend a penny; I stretched my legs by walking to and fro in the small clearing near the ladder and I said to myself, "The prisoner is taking exercise in the yard."

I'm really fed up to the ears with this rhino affair. I suppose that there are some people who, if in my place, wouldn't leave without at least seeing a rhino—the same kind of people who once they try to climb a mountain must get to the top. I have some of that spirit, but I'm grateful it's within reason. Last year I climbed Kilimanjaro, for part of the ABC film on Africa. I made it to about 17,500 feet, and then my heart began to palpitate too much. At that point I was climbing five minutes and resting flat on my back for ten. I was somewhat stronger in 1959 when I reached the Margherita Glacier on the Ruwenzori. One pleasure—there aren't many—in climbing those African mountains is the way in which plant life changes as you gain altitude. You begin in the tropics but by the time you have reached about 7,000 feet, you are in the temperate zone and you see plants found in Maine, like the bracken fern. This continues to the snow line, where you're not surprised to find Alpine immortelles. Udjong Kulon is mostly sea level; there are some high hills, but no mountains. I might add our scene here below the tree house is dark enough without rain.

Last night, and several times before, Effendy, who knows of my extensive work in Africa, asked me to compare Udjong Kulon with African sanctuaries. This isn't easy. Here, as in Africa, the climate is tropical. Many of the wild animals found here are found in Africa too. But Africa has many areas, like the parks in Uganda, Kenya, and Tanzania that are mostly open grassland with just a few trees. In these areas you can approach almost any animal with freedom provided you are in a Land Rover, for the beasts ignore vehicles.

Udjong Kulon does not have the tallest or thickest forest I have seen. I dislike calling it a rain forest, although Lee Talbot calls it that, since it does not rain that much, or every day. The

284

Ituri in the east Congo is a real rain forest, with heavy trees and thick underbrush; there not a single ray of light penetrates the unbroken mass of foliage above. Here in Udjong Kulon, as I think I've said earlier in this diary, it is the incredible number of plants with thorns that most impresses one. The rattans in particular have continuous sets of what appear to be sharp fishhooks. These catch hold in taller trees, which the rattans then climb fifty or more feet to reach the sun.

It's stopped raining, but is extremely humid. Every metal object I have here, except for those of stainless steel, is covered with rust. I wonder what the insides of my Nikons look like. Two of my cameras are out of action and four of my exposure meters are dead. It's a lucky thing people don't rust, or do we?

Amazingly enough, I still feel fine and very fit. I am still down two inches at the waist, and I haven't taken an aspirin except once for a sore throat, or a Miltown, or a sleeping pill. I think I have four sleeping pills with me, for night travel on jets. Except they get there so fast now.

2:30. Anda, with his superacute senses, just heard the engine of the *Harini*.

3:30. No rhino. No animals of any kind. Also, no more rain. No more anything except annoyance.

Seems a pity to end an exciting assignment, and a major episode in my life, on this negative note. There's only tomorrow left, and possibly the next morning.

Perhaps the Schenkels did photograph a rhino; I hope so. I'll know in about an hour and a half, when Effendy gets here.

Tuesday, October 31

Don't know the correct time. My watch is off again. Judging from the sun, which is almost high enough to light the river, it's about 10 A.M.

Last evening Effendy delivered two fat envelopes of mail brought by the *Harini* from Labuan. They were dated October 16 and 19. Not too bad for communications, considering where I am.

A letter each from Elin and Jill. Dotty Scher, my secretary, sent a sheaf of TV columns about ABC's Africa show, which was an extraordinary success. I was given kudos for the color photography—too many kudos, since I didn't do too much more than select the film we all used, a new high-speed Kodak film that was still unproved, and help to pick some of the camera crews. More credit should have gone to the men who were in the field—men like Jerry Feil, one of America's most talented cameramen, who was never mentioned. My credit, Director of Creative Production, was rather ambiguous. No one knew what to call me. I helped with the formulation of the show, including bringing in my friend Robert Ardrey, and I went to Africa twice: the first time to produce-direct the animal and the land sequences, and the second to do the Congo. Quibbles aside, I'm happy the show was such a success.

The *Badak* stopped at the beach camp yesterday morning, and the Schenkels returned my underwater camera and reported they still had no pictures of a rhino. They heard one two nights ago, and yesterday Rudei chased one but wasn't able to photograph it.

I still think that here in this thick jungle, where you sometimes can't see farther than five yards, you must wait for the animal to come to you. The Schenkels were here earlier than I was, when it was still wet; they tracked and saw several rhinos, but took no pictures because the animals were so obscured. Mrs. Schenkel has said that now she'd photograph even one leg of a rhino if it showed. Too bad. It's such an old rule in photography, shoot first and worry afterward about the quality. You can always discard a picture when you have a better one.

Dotty Scher wrote that she's been finding the diary segments I've been sending her fascinating. This is encouraging, since her opinion counts a lot with me. She also thinks there's a safari handbook in the material. That doesn't particularly appeal to me. It is possible that a publisher will be interested in a diary with a hundred pictures or so. Unfortunately, I've done very little in black and white. It's possible to convert color pictures, but not always too well. We'll see.

It rained for several hours last night. Some water dripped in—just enough to wake me and keep me fitfully awake thinking about the mail and listening to the noise of the rain. This morning it's bright and sunny. Only a few birds are stirring. Nothing else.

Don't have much hope of seeing a rhino today—my last chance, since I asked Effendy to send Djaja in the big canoe late this afternoon so Anda and I can make our exit. Back to the tower tomorrow morning to begin the odious job of packing camping gear, camera equipment, and personal belongings. The camping stuff must be packed so it can be stored as is until the time comes to use it again. That won't be soon I hope. I crossed the Congo Basin this year, and now Udjong Kulon—this should last me for at least another year. I love nature and outdoor life; I even have hopes of living in Maine at least four months each year, when I can afford to; but I was born in Manhattan, and I'm still very urban.

In the mail yesterday there was an encouraging letter from Jim Lawrence, the vital force behind the American Institute of Architects plan to produce a series of films explaining the history of architecture. Two years ago I directed a pilot film for

286

wind is very shifty today. The animals keep stopping and taking stock. They know something is around, but don't know where.

I think it's been a month since I was last in this blind. Sometimes we don't appreciate what we have until it's gone. It's not that way here. I know how great this is, and I am drinking every last drop. I'll be able to taste it again and again for a very long time.

Glossary of Fauna

BIRDS

Chestnut-headed bee-eater   (*Merops viridis*)
Green peacock   (*Pavo muticus*)
Little cormorant   (*Phalacrocorax niger*)
Little egret   (*Egretta garzetta*)
Pied hornbill   (*Anthracoceros malabaricus*)
Reef heron   (*Egretta sacia*)
Rhinoceros hornbill   (*Buceros rhinoceros*)
Wreathed hornbill   (*Rhyticeros undulatus*)

MAMMALS

Banteng   (*Bos sondaicus*)
Barking deer   (*Cervulus muntjac*)
Flying lemur   (*Galeopterus variegatus*)
Fruit bat   (*Pteropus vampyrus*)
Gibbon   (*Hylobates moloch*)
Javan rhinoceros   (*Rhinoceros sondaicus*)
Leopard   (*Panthera pardus*)
Monkey   (*Macaca irus*)
Mouse deer   (*Tragulus javanicus*)
Rusa deer   (*Cervus timorensis*)
Squirrel   (*Ratufa bicolor*)
Wild dog   (*Cuon javanicus*)
Wild pig   (*Sus vittatus*)

REPTILES AND AMPHIBIANS

Agamid lizard   (*Calotes jubatus*)
Crocodile   (*Crocodylus porosus*)
Frog   (*Rhacophorus sp.*)
Monitor lizard   (*Varanus salvator*)
Python   (*Python reticulatus*)
Skink   (*Mabuia multifasciata*)

FISH

Barracuda   (*Sphyraena sp.*)
Eagle ray   (*Aetobatus sp.*)
False albacore   (*Euthynnus affinis*)
King mackerel   (*Scomberomorus guttatus*)
Mudskipper   (*Periopthalmus affinis*)

INSECTS

Cockoo wasp   (*Stilbum sp.*)
Walking stick   (Phasmatidae Family)

Index